LOVE AND COURAGE

LOVE AND COURAGE

A Story of Insubordination

O

Pregs Govender

Ipas Resource Center

First published by Jacana Media (Pty) Ltd in 2007

10 Orange Street
Sunnyside
Auckland Park 2092
South Africa
(+27 11) 628-3200
www.jacana.co.za

ISBN 978-1-77009-342-3

Set in Goudy 12/16pt
Printed by CTP Books
Job No. 000441

See a complete list of Jacana titles at www.jacana.co.za

This book is dedicated to

Parusha, Yashodan and Saien: your courage as you forge your own paths with love, humour and clarity inspired me to be true to myself in the writing of this book.

Paul: for breaking the mould, as father and step-father, for long walks in the forest, for your meticulous eye, and for your love and support.

The reader: this book is woven together from my diaries, notebooks, papers and memory and checked, as far as possible, against the memory of others, from their recorded and unrecorded history and herstory. I hope that my book will inspire you to write down your memories, your stories.

CONTENTS

੧

PART 2 – POLITICS

PART 3 – POWER

PART 4 – CHOICES

PART 5 – THE ARMS DEAL

PART 6 – NO HIV/AIDS

9

INTRODUCTION

February 1994 was a time of personal and political change, a time of letting go of the old and entering the new. It was a busy period for me. The campaign I had managed for the Women's National Coalition, from its headquarters in Johannesburg, was complete and a national conference was scheduled to wrap up the process. South Africa was on course towards its first democratic elections and I had been nominated onto the African National Congress list of candidates to parliament, situated in Cape Town. I was going to move there with my two children and the man I loved to build a life together. I had also seen a lawyer about securing a divorce from my first husband, from whom I had been separated for many years.

During this time I accepted an invitation to attend an international leadership conference in India entitled the Mount Abu Leadership Dialogue. The invitation to the Dialogue struck a chord in me: I knew I needed to go. Although it was for only a few days, I felt it would be important for me to go there, to learn, to reflect and to consolidate.

At Bombay airport the heat hit me in waves. I was inappropriately dressed in jeans, socks, tackies and my daughter Parusha's colourful warm jacket, unlike my guide, who visited India regularly and was dressed far more sensibly in a light, white sari. In Bombay we settled into our accommodation, before visiting the home of a senior member of my guide's spiritual organisation. While they discussed lessons from their morning's meditation, I noticed a little girl working hard in the kitchen. She did not join us when we ate, unlike the relative of our host. When I asked who she was, the translated response was, 'She is God's child.' My guide explained that she was a street-child our host took care of. I looked at the child and saw unpaid child labour. 'What exactly does being "God's child" mean?' I retorted. I thought of my brother Pat passionately arguing that 'India needs a good dose of communism to get rid of all the superstitious bullshit'.

Far from home and family, my guide and I walked through the crowded streets back to our accommodation. Amid the homes of rags and cardboard, the sight of a little girl brushing her teeth on the pavement stopped me in my tracks. I am not sure if it was her sheer determination not to be defeated by her surroundings or the hopefulness of her act that pierced all my defences. I was missing my daughter Parusha and my son Yashodan, was exhausted from the flight and shocked at the vast scale of the poverty. It was my first experience of India, the home my ancestors had left as indentured labourers to become virtual slaves to South Africa's sugar barons. I began to cry and my guide tried to comfort me: 'Pregs, they are fine, really. They are detached from their suffering. They understand that in this reincarnation, it is their karma.' All I could see was a child surrounded by poverty and the answer infuriated me. In the streets of Bombay, my guide and I shouted at each other as we argued, beginning our rough ride to close friendship.

That night I remembered the story of a guru and his disciple. When a bridge collapsed at a religious function, killing many

people, a young disciple asked his guru why they had died. He expected an explanation of karmic laws, the usual gross reduction of political, economic and social causes. Instead, the guru shook his head and said, 'Ah, my son, it was a combination of poor engineering and bad planning.'

At one of the hosting organisation's centres in India, a 'senior sister' asked me where my ancestors came from. Prior to my trip I had never experienced any sense of yearning to visit India. I identified myself as a South African, did not see India as my 'motherland' and did not know which village my family came from, although I had been told they were from the south. When I answered her question, she shook her head with disbelief and said disparagingly, 'South Indians are black, like Africans.' South Indians, descendants of the Dravidians, had been conquered by fair-skinned Aryans in one of India's first colonisations. Although the demarcation by colour is not so clearly evident anymore, prejudice is deeply engrained and rigorously maintained even by South Indians, particularly high-caste Brahmins. This kind of prejudice against people who are dark-skinned was very familiar to me from my own country.

What shocked me most was experiencing such prejudice in a 'spiritual' person. The 'senior sister' insisted that my name, Pregaluxmi, an Indian name as far as I knew, did not exist. In a distinctly superior tone she explained that it was an incorrect spelling of Pregya, which means 'wisdom'. Later, when we requested a bath, she called my guide aside and spoke to her in Hindi while I was asked to wait outside the door. I did not try to argue about the prejudice implied in who could or could not use which bathroom. Trying to communicate this without the basic tool of Hindi, which I do not speak, was impossible.

I knew that every morning these good sisters meditated on human virtues such as respect, tolerance and love, and made deeply sincere efforts to transform themselves. But they live in, and to a

large degree accept, the system of caste which, like the system of apartheid I had lived in, was designed to take away the dignity of the human soul and to crush its joy and power. In India, caste is expressed in minor mundane acts of prejudice alongside profound inequities of access to good education, employment and property. This is a country in which 'untouchable' Hindus have been killed because their shadows crossed those of upper-caste Brahmins, who claim to respect life so much that they refuse to eat meat.

Nelson Mandela had been invited to the Dialogue but had declined. As I came into contact with India's caste prejudice, I felt glad that Madiba was not there to experience any of it. In that moment, I felt enormously proud of our movement and our inspired leader who had emerged from 27 years in prison with love not just as his philosophy but as a tangible quality that radiates from his being. In a letter from Robben Island to his wife Winnie, when she was imprisoned yet again by the apartheid state, he shared the practice he had developed in prison to keep his heart and soul intact. Advising regular daily meditation as a way of learning to know oneself, he stressed the importance in personal growth of nurturing qualities like honesty, sincerity, simplicity, humility, generosity and readiness to serve humanity, 'qualities within the reach of every soul ... Never forget that a saint is a sinner that keeps on trying.' In his letter, Madiba does not mention god or religion but talks of spirituality. His words reinforced my understanding of spirituality as the practice of evoking the best in the human spirit, so as to fully appreciate all of life.

En route to our destination on Mount Abu in the state of Rajasthan, we had to wind our way through some of India's largest and busiest cities, filled with cows, loud hooting and many temples. Religion was everywhere, in the temples, churches and mosques. Most of India's people are 'Hindu', the catch-all term for

the people and beliefs that the Aryan colonisers found in ancient cities like Harappa and along the banks of the River Indus.

In South Africa I grew up knowing two types of Hindu. There were the men and women who prayed regularly, and observed custom, diet and dress. They had many pictures of deities or Gandhi on the walls of their homes and shops in Durban's Grey Street complex. They talked of karma as the basis of their good fortune, not the fact that they paid low wages and exploited their Indian and African workers. Such Hindus used detachment to explain and justify their complacency even as they established numerous religious institutions. Theirs was truly the religion of the moneyed classes.

Growing up, I had also known Hindus who may or may not have used the term 'Hindu' as a description of parentage or place of origin. They placed emphasis on the practice of good in action and refused to be complacent in the face of injustice and suffering. Detachment for them was the ability to transform negative emotions so as to act more resolutely and effectively with love. I saw in them a deep self-respect and a respect for every other human being as well as a tolerance that every path to truth has validity and no one can claim that theirs is the only path. This type of Hindu may or may not have had the pictures, the institutions or the customs. Yet, their practice of these basic values fundamentally influenced me.

As I travelled through India, on planes and buses and India's very own auto-rickshaws, I had time to reflect on my topic for the Dialogue, 'Leadership: empowering the self and others', and my focus question, 'What was the role of love and courage in empowering me? How do I empower myself?' What had inspired and sustained my belief in the power of love and courage? What had enabled a young child, living with her family in a garage after being evicted from her home by apartheid's Group Areas Act, to write in a school essay that she would change the world starting

with the poverty of India? Was it because she was an egotistical little upstart or because she was able to dream, hope and believe, no matter what the circumstances?

As a child I was not fond of performing the rituals expected of good little Hindu girls. Once, when my mother scolded me for refusing to clean the family lamp because I wanted to play with my brothers instead, my grandmother intervened to defend me: 'She has a good heart and that is all that matters.' Her simple, authoritative words laid the basis for a spiritual understanding and practice in my life: belief in the potential, power and practice of love. Through her love for me, my grandmother taught me how love nurtures the best in the human spirit. I was inspired by this as I parented my children and in my work: to help people discover their own power, love and respect for themselves and each other, while developing the courage to act so as to change our world individually and collectively.

From Rajasthan, the road to our final destination was steep, narrow and winding with suicidal drivers and buses adorned with gods and signs saying 'Horn Please'. My stomach had relocated by the time we reached the top of the mountain. On the campus of the Brahma Kumaris World Spiritual University, everyone was dressed in white. We, the invited guests, were conspicuous in our coloured clothes. There were people from every continent, yet most of the guests were 'white' and there were no 'black Africans'.

I first made contact with the woman who was the driving force behind the university in the West, Dadi Janki, shortly after we had arrived and settled into spotlessly clean rooms. In the courtyard where everyone gathered, a short, grey-haired woman was seated on a white plastic chair. Her hair was wet and she had a fresh twinkle in her eye and a rose in her hand. She gestured in my direction and I wondered whom she was beckoning forward. 'It's

you she wants,' people around me said, smiling. I had been quietly observing everything and moved forward hesitantly. The 78-year-old woman looked deeply into my eyes as she handed me the rose and I felt the vision, the vibrations of good, and the breadth of her spirituality. As her love streamed to me, the discrimination and small-mindedness I had encountered from some members of her university fell away – those who had self-righteously perpetuated 'the soul versus the body', 'heaven above and hell below' and 'white as purity versus black as evil' as opposing, irreconcilable dichotomies.

It's a familiar fact: all too often the wisdom of inspired leaders is distorted by followers who stay trapped within worn-out paradigms. In contrast, Dadi Janki laughed and danced, and every morning walked energetically around the campus. In her room were photos of her young self with the other women yogis, vigorous-looking women in khaki shorts who had just finished exercising. Janki, who describes herself as a life-long student, rejects guru-dom. Comfortable in herself, she has clear boundaries which emerge from the deep self-respect she teaches: 'Humility must never be confused with a lack of self-esteem. While I would never impose myself on others, I would never allow others to impose themselves on me.'

On the first day of the Dialogue, after listening to several presenters from other countries, I walked up the mountain to watch the sun set. In the silence I meditated on the power of love within ourselves. With such power we can evoke our original qualities of peace and joy and recognise that these qualities are intrinsic to every one of us; with such power we can help transform our world. I know that when I forget this power and become consumed with fear, I become self-destructive. But when I focus my mind away from its incessant chatter and become aware of the power of love within myself, creativity and courage emerge, connecting me to myself and to others.

I do not like the language of God, entrapped within its very specific historical and cultural context. But I do appreciate the call – whoever makes it – to respect the love that resides within every human being when we ourselves may have completely lost sight of it. It is this recognition that characterises encounters with people like Madiba or Dadi Janki. Simply by being in their presence I feel elevated, even when they have not said a word. As someone who struggles at times to remain connected to the joy within myself, it is a gift to encounter it in children or in someone who has mastered the practice.

During the Dialogue I listened to leaders in the fields of politics, business, science and the media. I enjoyed meditating in silence, in groups and on my own, and walking around the beautiful campus. I had never had to present a public speech that demanded such a personal response, and eventually decided not to duck the challenge, not to betray the slogan of the international women's movement, 'The personal is political.' One morning I walked in a different direction and stood on an overhanging rock. The sun was just beginning to rise and the sky looked magnificent. Below me I heard the sound of a baby crying and a woman hushing it before she began to sweep and light a fire. I realised that her home was beneath the rock I was standing on. I smelt the smoke and heard a man gargling and spitting. As I walked away, I reflected on trying to transform old paradigms of politics, sexuality and spirituality, while taking care of the everyday joys and drudgeries of children and home. Seeking balance between the mundane and the sacred is not an easy path.

It took a long time before I finally wrote my presentation late into the night. In the massive gathering in the huge hall the next morning, I was nervous and needed to sit down. I could not talk off the cuff, without my notes. My starting point was the huge

challenge we would face in South Africa after our first democratic elections. How would we combine love and power, both essential to change the world and address the suffering of people? How would we develop leaders of vision and inspiration, of humility and dignity? How would we ensure creative, responsive and effective systems, not dull and deadened bureaucracies? I shared my belief that there was hope in the power of good and in the human spirit. I adapted Amilcar Cabral's wonderful saying, 'Tell no lies, claim no easy victories', adding 'in the battle of the soul or of the world'.

I also raised my criticisms openly and respectfully, including those about the hosting organisation such as the lack of participation by black Africans, the prejudice of caste that I'd encountered, and the use of concepts such as karma to justify exploitation. My heart melted when the small, grey-haired women in their bright white saris joyfully joined in a standing ovation. The director of President Clinton's national performance review of government, Carolyn Lukensmeyer, came onto the stage at the same time as a Russian scientist. 'Thank you,' they both said, in very different accents.

I was overwhelmed and needed to settle down quietly, on my own. There were many beautiful places in the vicinity, such as the large, wild rocks where leopards are said to roam at night. There I sat and watched the sun set amid vistas of mountain ranges, plains and valleys.

In the silence of my mind, I danced joyously, up and up the walls of a beautiful temple. Where there should have been the dome was the sky, onto which I danced ecstatically. I suddenly became aware that I was dancing on air, that there was nothing solid beneath my feet. I thought I was going to fall, when I heard a calm, reassuring voice from deep within myself: 'Don't worry, Pregaluxmi. Trust yourself.'

PART I

Life

One

ROOTS

Kamalam carried her baby through the worst months of Durban's humid summer. In the early dawn, she brought her child into the world.

On the morning you were born, I had a vivid dream. I used to take my mother her coffee in the morning before I went to school. In my dream I was wearing my white school uniform. I accidentally bumped my stomach on her big old brass bed. I cried that it hurt too much for me to go to school. She comforted me as I cried. In my dream I cried so loudly that I woke myself and everyone else.

I was actually in labour and crying from the pain. Dad [my mother calls my father 'Dad', perhaps because her father died when she was a just a few years old] rushed me to hospital. I was supposed to have a 'Caesar' because you had gone into a breech position the week before. I asked the nurse to take me to the labour ward. She was very rude and told me that I must 'just sit down and wait until we call

you'. You know how nurses can be. They would slap you if you screamed with pain.

I knew you were about to arrive, so I ignored the nurse and waddled off to find an empty bed. Those labour beds are so high – you have to jump onto them. Within a matter of minutes you made your way out. You couldn't wait. I don't know how you did it – the doctor had planned for the Caesarean – you were my miracle baby. The nurse came in time to cut the cord.

Kamalam's description downplays her role and power in giving me life. It does not mention the death of her own mother five days before I was born. What focus did it take for Kamalam to shift her consciousness out of mourning to welcome the birth of her daughter as a 'miracle'? Kamalam has light brown eyes, straight white teeth, small ears, high cheekbones and straight black hair that falls softly onto her shoulders. I used to look at myself and think that I had big ears and protruding Bugs Bunny teeth, in comparison to my mother, the most beautiful woman I knew.

One of the first rituals, the naming ceremony, was delayed by the choice of a suitable name. There was controversy around the name that my father had chosen. My father, Sathieseelan Gurulingam, whose first name, Sathie, means 'Truth', had been registered in apartheid days as Ronald by a well-meaning uncle, and forever bears the name Ronnie. He had joined male and female names together to create my name. Prega, 'One who overcomes all obstacles', is a male name, not normally bestowed on a girl, which Dad joined with the female Luxmi, 'Love'. While the dispute was being resolved, my father's oldest sister, Goonam, unwittingly gave me a nickname: 'my jewel, my little jewel'.

My father told me that Hindu newborns were often named after gods and goddesses in the belief that each one of us is unique and sacred. The *atman* – our infinitesimal, loving essence – is

at play in each of us; in all of life, according to him. My father's Hinduism, expressed as atheism in his youth, taught me that all human beings have infinite creative potential. It is in stark contrast to the bigotry of caste which characterises Hinduism in the land of our ancestors.

By the time I was in primary school I wished my father had chosen an easier name, especially when the teachers at St Anthony's Catholic School pursed their lips almost in disgust as they tried to pronounce it in anglicised accents. At St Anthony's I was taught that God was an old 'white' man who lived up in the sky, judging us and deciding whether we should go to heaven or hell. I was also taught that all human beings are born sinners, because of Eve's original sin. Baptism starts the process of cleansing and helps ensure that those who are baptised are saved from hell and damnation. I learnt that Hindus, like Africans, were 'heathens' – apartheid's version of the Arabic word was 'kaffirs'. Together with other heathens (who honoured each other, the ancestors, the earth and her creatures, the sun and the moon) I was destined to burn in hell's fires for all eternity. My ancestors were heathens whose traditional greeting 'Namaskaram' or 'Namaste' means 'The divine in me greets the divine in you'.

Generations of us, except those who came from India as indentured labourers like Dad's grandfather Veerasamy and Dad's grandmother, whose name no one can recall, have been captured on film by my father. He photographed his mother, my grandmother, whom I called Aya, on a trip to Cape Town. We had stopped at a beach somewhere; perhaps we parked next to it for the night. The sun was slowly coming up over the horizon. Aya was framed by the orange light, strands of her curly hair wild and free of her daytime bun. Her hands rose in prayer as she welcomed the day. Life and death cycled in the early morning as Aya's mantra took her into silence, and the sun lit the morning sky. It was an image and a practice which imprinted itself into my heart. I would silently repeat the mantra she

gave me before school exams and in the crises of adolescence. An invaluable legacy, her gift helped calm and focus me.

Aya, who was one of the founders of the Siva Alayum temple in Cape Town, taught me while I massaged her feet. I never became a temple-goer but I continue to hold Aya's powerful affirmations deep within me. She would tell me stories of tropical lands of mangoes, palm trees, beaches of warm water and white sand. The flowers of these paradisal lands were like none I had ever seen. I had to look up to them as they towered above me in their magnificence. She took me to see Indian films about gods and goddesses. I saw the famous movie *Mother India* with Aya. It was a film of monsoon rains, bloodletting on the scale of the River Ganges, and heartrending songs. I learnt about British colonialism, the role of Gandhi in the movement against colonialism, the Independence of India, and the terrible conflicts between Muslims and Hindus over the partition – the policy of divide and rule which is played out across the world. I wept as I watched the film. It was years later that I learnt that South Africa was the birthplace of Gandhi's powerful philosophy of satyagraha. Brought to South Africa by Indian businessmen to protect their interests, Gandhi initially expressed prejudice against Africans and indentured labourers, who formed the majority of Indians. It was South Africans like 15-year-old Velliama Mudaliar, who literally died because of the courage of her convictions, that helped inspire and shape satyagraha as the 'force born out of truth, love and non-violence'.

As a gentle matriarch in her community, Aya helped establish the Rylands Hindu Women's Association. A photo of all the members in their white saris gave me a sense of continuity with her impulse to unite with other women. In Aya's world, girls and women were expected to be quietly subordinate – there were few areas in which to claim and express power. One of the ways in which Aya expressed power was through trance. She would dance a wild dance with protruding tongue and wide-open eyes.

She would breathe deeply, her voice resonating from the womb, shaking the ground as she stamped her feet and blew ash onto us. Around her, everyone would start singing, as if their harmony would hold her safely through her journey. I was filled with fear and fascination. I watched Aya closely and learnt of the power of life which created, sustained and destroyed, the power she called Shakti. I learnt of the silence from which Shakti emerges and to which Shakti returns, which she called Shiva. Like her ancestors, Aya was a Shaivite, a devotee of Shiva, who manifested in diverse forms. From Aya, I learnt of the dance of Shiv Shakti, at play in each of us, in all of life, as we dance the universe into being.

I observed these powers in those around me. I loved the silence and the dance but was fearful of the destruction of Kali, evoked by Durga's fury at the evil that was destroying her creation and threatening humanity. It would be years before I learnt that it was fine for a woman to use her power against injustice, wherever it occurred. On Aya's small shrine there was a cobra around the neck of Shiva. I learnt that the cobra symbolised the potential for transformation that exists within each of us. It is the kundalini energy that rises from our base chakra to our crowns, creating wholeness. For St Anthony's Catholic School, the serpent was evil. He tempted Eve, who ate the forbidden fruit and became the temptress, causing the downfall of Adam and of all humanity.

My father's camera captured many moments of joy in our childhood. At five years old, I was unaware that anyone was watching as I picked a rose from my mother's garden in Spearman Road and buried my face in it. As my mother came into view I quickly hid the rose behind my back. Ma looked as if she was scolding me as the film zoomed in on her face. While she walked away, the camera turned to me as I defiantly brought my rose out of hiding, smelt it, and made a face at Ma's departing back.

Dad's camera also caught my grandfather Dorasamy, my Thatha, looking dignified whether in shorts or suit, his hat nattily perched

on his head. My brother Daya inherited the dignity of his eyes and being. Thatha didn't drink alcohol, unlike his sons in their adulthood, and he did not approve of bullshitting. Thatha had a reputation for not kowtowing to the *baas* (Afrikaans for a 'white' boss) unlike many Indians. He didn't tolerate bullies and thugs of any colour. In our family, his exploits demolished the stereotyped Indian. It was hard to imagine Thatha or his ancestors being subservient to any slave-owner or sugar-cane baron. There's a photo of Thatha in the Bakers' Trade Union, of which he was a member. I look at it and think that perhaps his trade unionism was an inspiration for my own passion for the trade union I served as an adult.

Thatha was warm and gentle to us, his grandchildren. I know that my father and his brothers had felt the back of Thatha's hand and the sting of his belt. But we knew only gentleness as we put our tiny hands in his. I thought he was the handsomest man in the world and idolised him completely. Thatha and Aya had secretly written letters to each other after their first meeting, and contrary to convention, theirs had not been an arranged marriage.

At my ninth birthday party, Dad received the phone message that Thatha had been rushed to hospital. We packed my birthday cake and the colddrinks into the car and Dad rushed us to Cape Town. Daya, Pat and I did not understand that when Thatha died we would never see him again, that he would never again take us fishing or for drives in his car. A tent was put up for his funeral and one morning the three of us, with our other cousins, slid on it. The finality of his death did not register even when the coffin slid into the flames before the small door slammed shut.

When Thatha died, Aya had to stop wearing her *thali*, the yellow marriage string. She could no longer apply the red dot of a married woman, and had to start wearing the white sari of a widow. After a family prayer for Thatha, I went to school wearing ash on my forehead and was silently furious with the 'white' teacher who told me to rub it off. When Aya died, her body too was cremated and her ashes, like Thatha's, were scattered into the ocean.

Two

GROUNDING

Daya, my older brother and hero, made me laugh through our childhood while teaching me yoga and karate. He learnt yoga from a simple illustrated book and taught me the asanas as he experimented with them. They felt like an elaborate, interconnected dance. Yoga's stretching and breathing transformed me. I became a mountain rooted in the earth reaching the sky; a dog on all fours with my backside in the air; a tall tree balanced on one leg, my branches stretching out from deep within; a cat luxuriously arching its back; a cobra alert and ready to strike; a majestic lion with a full-throated roar; a graceful bird in full flight; a courageous warrior who was bow, arrow and target. When I finally sank into the earth I became a still, silent corpse.

I developed the flexibility of knee that was needed for yoga as I squatted over the hole in the ground – our 'eastern' toilet – or the bucket toilet at my cousin's home in Clare Estate. But I lost the central principle of breathing rhythmically when I watched the buckets being collected. I would hold my breath, hoping the buckets wouldn't spill their stinking contents on the men who

carried them. Instead of my father's favourite pose, the head stand, I revelled in the shoulder stand. Ma says that when I was born, the bones of my skull had not completely knitted into place, resulting in some sensitivity on top. I learnt later that this is true for almost all babies. At the time, it provided my brothers with good ammunition for jokes about my cracked head.

I learnt yoga easily with Daya. He made everything seem like a lot of fun – unlike the dragon Tamil class teacher we had when we were about 11 and 12 years old. We played truant to escape him and the humiliation of being the oldest and most ignorant Tamil students. Our humiliation was underscored by a five-year-old who recited the alphabet in Tamil without blinking or pausing for breath. 'Aana, avina ...' Daya and I did not remain in the class for long. Years later, at university, I studied and passed a course in Tamil. In lengthy discussions with the lecturer I learnt a great deal about Indian philosophy, but that was in English. Like Daya, I am still not conversant in Tamil.

In childhood, we moved home many times. Perhaps our first few moves established the nomadic pattern of my life ever since. Our family's first two moves were dictated by the Group Areas Act, which dislocated thousands of families and communities in South Africa. People were moved from Sophiatown, District Six and many other communities. By means of the law, the Nationalist government used race and ethnicity as the basis for division and discrimination. Cato Manor, the home of my parents, was declared South Africa's first group area under the Act. Using apartheid race classification, the government reserved Cato Manor for whites and forced out African, Indian and Coloured people.

Daya was born and I was conceived in Cato Manor. At an early age we became aware of the dreaded year 1949, the year that Indians in Cato Manor were attacked by Africans, with white policemen standing by, doing nothing to stop the rapes, beatings and murders. Ma, Dad, Aya, Thatha and the rest of their family survived. Dad

told us that while a number of Indians met their deaths, many others were rescued by Africans impelled by their belief in *ubuntu* (I am because you are; you are because we are). They risked their lives to save Indians from mob violence. Progressive historians later exposed the role of the state in the riots. They revealed that *agents provocateurs*, who provided transport, petrol and money for the attackers, were white men, blackened in disguise, and their black lackeys.

Our school history textbooks and the media entrenched the stereotype of the bloodthirsty, primitive African and the exploitative, money-grabbing Indian. My father, who was well read and had many books, recalled and shared his experience and insights, not just with our family but with a community whose memory of 'anti-Indian' violence made it vulnerable to manipulation. His play *1949* exposed state-sponsored vigilantism. The year 1949 was also a time of unity between Indians and Africans, symbolised by the famous Doctors' Pact, a joint commitment by the African National Congress and Natal Indian Congress to work together against apartheid, signed by three doctors who were leaders in our communities – Xuma, Dadoo and Naicker. Throughout apartheid's history, whenever non-racial unity was being forged, the state created so-called racial violence which 'coincidentally' flared at the same time.

The 1949 assaults explained Ma's initial fear of the dairy workers who raced into the garden of our family home in Spearman Road. I was playing outside when a stranger, an Indian man, rushed into our house and locked the front door. Grabbing our door keys he ran into the bathroom and locked himself in. He had stolen clothing off a washing line belonging to the dairy workers who lived at the top of our road. The workers chased after him with menacing pangas – huge knives used to cut bushes. My mother, fluent in seven languages including Zulu, was shocked into silence. Locked into her own home, she watched helplessly as

her friendly, bandy-legged toddler greeted the fierce-looking men warmly and began to talk to them. My mother recalls how her fear turned into pleasant surprise. The workers began to laugh and respond to her baby before the police finally arrived to arrest the man in our bathroom.

When our house in Spearman Road was declared part of a Coloured group area, it was difficult to find another home, so my parents, both teachers, moved to the only accommodation they could find at the time – someone's garage. In the garage I watched the ants walk purposefully up and down the windowsill in orderly lines. I looked for the rainbows after the rain had cleared. When it rained through the sunshine, Daya and I sang that 'the monkey and baboon are getting married'. I held red and black polka-dotted ladybirds in my hand and fervently made my wish. The nursery rhyme was tragic: 'Ladybird, ladybird, fly away home / Your house is on fire and your children are gone.' The rays of the sun caught flecks of dust, becoming worlds into which I swirled and danced. I disappeared into the silence, and the words of writers whose tales swept me away from parental fights, schoolyard bullies and Ma's commands to 'stop daydreaming'.

In the garage the rain came through the bottom of the door, wetting the space that was our bedroom, bathroom, kitchen and lounge. My older brother Daya became ill with bronchitis. Ma would come home and make chicken soup – she always made sure that we were well fed and warmly dressed. Daya began to have a daily 'egg-flip', a raw egg beaten with milk, nutmeg, cinnamon and sugar. Ma rubbed our chests, backs, foreheads and behind our ears with Vicks Vaporub. Her hands were soft and comforting. Dad volunteered to help but although I love him dearly, his hands were rough compared to Ma's.

Dad taught at the tuberculosis settlement, Friends of the Sick Association (Fosa), where he caught TB. A widespread disease amongst the poor, TB was feared because it could kill. The apartheid

government did not care, so people had to look after themselves and each other. Fosa was set up by the community to control the disease by teaching patients how to take their medication regularly, grow nutritious food, have enough rest and exercise, and prevent TB from spreading to other members of the family. A nurse who also worked at Fosa, Poomani Moodley, was a political activist in the ANC; she was detained and tortured by apartheid police in the 1950s. She was down to earth, unpatronising and direct. I liked her and got to know her better in the 1980s.

Dad, who had lost an eye in childhood, and kept his prosthetic eye in a cup next to his bed at night, was determined not to let TB get the better of him. Every morning he woke early and stood on his head before exercising energetically. In our garage Dad meticulously put his plate, cup and cutlery under the sink, away from our dishes. He was strict about resting. During lunch breaks at Fosa school he lay on a wooden bench and fell fast asleep, but woke promptly to teach his afternoon classes.

While my father battled with TB, I plotted to change the world. At home I kept secret diaries and wrote in them almost every day. In school the subject I loved most was writing, and when we were told to write on 'What will I be when I grow up?' I wrote the essay I would quote years later in India. Neither I nor any member of my family had visited India at that time, but we all knew that it had the largest number of poor people in the world. After solving India's poverty, I wrote that I was going to solve the poverty of South Africa and then the rest of the world.

Not content with all this, which would be complete by the time I was 40, I would adopt two children. After raising them, I would do yoga and reach nirvana at 60. In our garage, Daya read my audacious plan and laughed so much that his eyes watered. Pat, still too tiny to make sense of what was so funny, laughed along with Daya. My father, who let me dream wild, impossible dreams, was proud of my little essay. Throughout my childhood I heard the

night-time click-clacking of his typewriter as he wrote his sports columns and his plays. Wherever we lived, in a garage, a flat or a nice house in a middle-class suburb, and whatever his daytime job, whether teacher or salesman, the familiar sound of my father's typewriter at night, simultaneously comforting and irritating, conveyed the value and personal fulfilment of a writing life.

Dad, who worked hard at his two jobs as a journalist and teacher, knew that stress aggravated illness. Perhaps this was why he refused to stress quietly about the obnoxious landlord of the garage, who had no respect for our privacy. The landlord believed our home was part of the little fiefdom that was centred on his house on the corner of Abelia Road, and that he could walk into his garage whenever he wanted. My father angrily toppled his fiefdom by physically barring his entry while telling him loudly what he thought of his rude behaviour. Fortunately my mother timeously found another home.

In flat number 7, Joosab's Building, Sparks Road, Overport, my father and mother had their own bedroom. Still, the walls were paper-thin and I grew up reassured that my parents, despite all their fights, loved each other passionately. At night the lounge cum dining-room became our bedroom, the divan extending into a bed that Daya, Pat and I shared. When I reached puberty, Ma and Dad separated this room with a bookcase to create a space that became my very own room. In the 'eastern' toilet there was a container of water to wash in and Ma put neat squares of newspaper on wire, for us to wipe with. The bathroom was a small square of cement with a short border of bricks that prevented us splashing water all over. We filled the bucket with water and used the *chomboo*, a small container, to pour the water over ourselves. Outside the bathroom and toilet was a little space where Ma put a table. While we did our homework here, she marked her pupils' books and prepared her teaching lessons.

Ma, like Dad, loved books. They shared a love for good novels,

but she did not venture into his books on politics and philosophy. Dad had works by Bertrand Russell, Bertolt Brecht, Rabindranath Tagore and Tolstoy. As I grew, I delved into and enjoyed his favourite authors, only lamenting much later the dearth of female authors on his shelves. Ma studied throughout our childhood trying to improve her education. She wrote Afrikaans exams to better her qualifications as an Afrikaans teacher. Unlike other teachers, she tutored children free of charge. As an adult, I met a teacher who felt 'eternal gratitude' to my mother for tutoring him in Afrikaans, a subject compulsory for passing matric. He had failed his matric exams twice before he came to her for help, and passed on his third try.

Ma taught at St Aidan's School in Sparks Road. One day, while on scholar patrol duty, the child holding the stop sign was thrown into the air by a speeding car. The child fell down in front of Ma and she was holding him when he died. Ma was angry, upset that the driver believed that he could get away with it because he was rich and white. Contrary to her instinctive reactions, my mother was wary of 'politics', fearful of its consequences for her family. But on this occasion her outrage was so great, she went to court to testify against the driver. He was freed, despite her determination.

Against Ma's wishes, Dad encouraged Daya, Pat and me to be critical of the society we lived in, to discuss and debate politics. While we were in Joosab's Building, Dad stopped being a schoolteacher. He was a troublemaker with a big mouth, which Ma wished he would keep shut. Troublemakers could not remain teachers for the Indian Affairs education department. When he was thrown out, he began working for South African Breweries as a salesman. After that there was always beer in the flat. I hated it when my father's friends sat around the table drinking and arguing late into the night. Dad also loved music, everything from Indian Carnatic music to jazz, and would sometimes spontaneously break

into song and dance. All I wanted was for the talking and the music to stop and for his friends to leave so I could go to sleep. Ma also did not like the commotion and would fight with Dad about this. She was very clear that children had to have a strict routine of early to bed, early to rise. At the time I did not appreciate my father's friends and their discussions. One of the visitors, Rick Turner, was assassinated by the state for his role in the labour movement. He was a leading intellectual of the trade unions of the 1970s and the famous Durban strikes.

Dad's love for film led him to buy a home projector on which he would show us Charlie Chaplin movies. All the children in the flat and the neighbourhood would crowd together on the floor and roar with laughter. There was a lot of falling face down into flour bags, slipping on wet floors or banana peels, and pies in faces. In Chaplin's fights there was never any blood, unlike the regular Friday night fights in Sparks Road, where there was always blood. In those years Saths Cooper and Strini Moodley, friends of my father's and active in the Black Consciousness Movement, borrowed Dad's projector. At the time I felt resentment that the fun of Charlie Chaplin and the movie gatherings of our friends ended. However, by the time Saths and Strini were arrested and sent to Robben Island, the projector had completely faded from memory.

Pat, my little brother, was the beauty of our family, with big brown eyes and long eyelashes. I grew close to Pat in late adolescence and came to appreciate him fully in adulthood. When he was a toddler, he demanded something I was holding at the window from which we had just waved Dad goodbye. Irritated, I threw it out and said, 'Here, if you want it, go and get it.' I had not thought he would actually jump after it. He dived head first and knocked himself unconscious on the cement driveway. The doctor said he had serious concussion. I was guilt-stricken as I hung my head in shame for being such a horrible big sister. People came in

and out praying for Pat. The aunties in the flats said prayers to Christ, to Allah, to Krishna, to whomever they believed in. Pat did not stir. Dad arrived, went straight to our family lamp, lit it, and sat in silence, before gently speaking to Pat. 'My baby. Pat, it's Dad, wake up, my baby.' Pat opened his eyes, smiled, and kissed my father. I began to breathe again.

Unlike me, Daya was gentle and kind to Pat and to myself. When the rain fell and filled the gutter, Daya taught us how to make paper boats and we would set sail on high seas. When the wind blew, he taught us how to make kites out of paper and bamboo, and I was filled with wonder at how high our little kites would fly above us. Out of tin cans he taught us to make a telephone; I would run round the corner of the flat, delighted at hearing Pat's and Daya's voices emerge from the ordinary-looking tin can. On our trips to the beach Daya taught Pat and me the lyrics of songs, and we beat out the rhythm on biscuit tin lids as we sang along.

Daya was the typical all-round achiever who won prizes for everything, from schoolwork to athletics. At home, he was very popular with all the boys and girls in the flat, and they would join us in the game of hoopoo, a game like baseball. Angered at losing, a boy who liked kicking and hitting the girls in the flats one day raised his leg to kick me. He was unaware that I had learnt some useful karate moves from Daya. I caught his leg in mid-air and held on tight: 'Say you will never kick another girl again, say it!' His father owned a karate dojo and he did karate. He was red, angry, swearing. 'Say sorry,' I insisted. Almost in tears, this boy – much larger and stronger than me – mumbled that he would never do this again, not to any girl.

Although I was a girl, I went with my brothers to the boxing matches my father compèred. I learnt about and loved Daya's hero Cassius Clay (Muhammad Ali), who was jailed for refusing to fight in America's war against Vietnam. We all learnt his chant, 'Float

like a butterfly, sting like a bee.' We stayed up listening to the radio commentary when Ali came to Zaire for the 'Rumble in the Jungle'. But the sight of men beating each other's brains out made my stomach curdle, so I quickly opted out of watching boxing matches. The last one I went to starred the very handsome 'Tap Tap' Makhatini, who was quite a legend in Durban.

In Durban, summer time was holiday time. In the heat of the day we would walk to a swimming pool near us, in the suburb of Asherville, where we played for hours before returning home late in the afternoon. Swimming always made us hungry and hot. We would eat luscious mangoes, watermelons, litchis and sticky jackfruit; the juice would run down our chins as we sucked into the sweetness. Daya and his friends would chase after sugar-cane trucks and grab long sticks of the cane. We would chew the sweetness from the sticks until they were dry and the strands would remain stuck in our teeth. At night, little ant-like creatures – we called them 'essels' – grew wings and hundreds fluttered around the glow of each streetlight in Sparks Road. We chased and caught them in glass jars.

But we stopped running around in our shortie pyjamas when we became aware that there were gangsters at the street corners, released after little or no time in jail. The police and the courts did not take rape seriously in our area. The police came quickly only when they wanted to add to the violence of Sparks Road. Their loud whistles would pierce the normal everyday noises and people would start shouting and screaming, 'The blackjacks are here.' African domestic workers, drivers or packers in the shops would run frantically for cover to hide in washing baskets, under beds, in toilets. There were no search warrants for the 'dompas' – the blackjacks kicked open doors and dragged out screaming whomever they found, beating wildly with their batons. There were tears, howls of pain, pleading, and the occasional resistance that was quickly subdued.

While we were living in Joosab's Building, my mother discovered my father was having an affair. It seemed to propel her into cooking, cleaning and parenting with a vengeance. In these years my parents' fighting intensified and my mother reverted to her aunt's authoritarian approach to raising children. All her anger and helplessness from childhood to adulthood erupted in pure rage. Every one of the children I knew in Joosab's Building and most of my cousins received 'hidings' from their mothers. Parents wielding the belt on little children was the norm. Now my mother joined in. I nursed huge, helpless anger and wrote it down in my secret diaries. I was determined never to do the same. The resistance grew in my eyes and it infuriated Ma. 'You stubborn, stubborn child!' Ma, beautiful and intelligent, had nowhere to take her youthfulness and intelligence, outside teaching and parenting. At home there was a lot to contend with, which just made matters worse. Ma had to do daily battle with the ever-encroaching stench of the garbage, the rats, mice and huge flying cockroaches, from the communal bin area next to our flat.

Ma insisted on everything being kept scrupulously clean, food being covered, and dishes being washed immediately. When I married, I had to fight this almost genetic intolerance of untidiness in myself that too easily undercut my stand for an equal sharing of housework. Dad loved to cook and in the process made a mess in the kitchen, which was Ma's domain. I enjoyed whatever he cooked, whether *karavad* (dried fish) chutney, fried sardines from Durban's 'sardine run', chops or mushroom curry. Ma was less appreciative, perhaps because she was the one for whom cooking was the daily chore, not the occasional choice. She cleaned up after my father's culinary adventures, as his cleaning never met her standards.

Ma's best friend, Aunty Julie, was a slim, attractive, feisty woman. They shared many secrets. My mother told her about my father's affair with the woman who was her friend. I did not like

the fact that she discussed family matters with outsiders. Of course all the neighbours heard my parents fight, but when the next day dawned I hoped that no one had heard anything. Society's rule 'Don't wash your dirty linen in public' had already seeped into my heart; for years it would shame me into silence. Aunty Julie was divorced by her husband. 'Talaq, talaq, talaq: I divorce you, I divorce you, I divorce you, and no maintenance for the children,' she would laugh wryly.

She and my mother shared the small joys of smoking cigarettes and playing fah-fee. 'Decent' Indian women were not supposed to smoke, drink, wear pants and short dresses, but radical, insubordinate women like Dr Goonam and Poomani Moodley led the way, merrily ignoring society's injunctions. One day Aunty Julie's daughter Banu took her mother's cigarette packet and passed a lit cigarette around our group of friends. I coughed, choked and envied the ease of the others, who breathed easily, even blowing the smoke out in shapes. If Aunty Julie had caught Banu she would have beaten her with whatever came to hand, a broom or a shoe. Aunty Julie's and my mother's other joy was fah-fee, a Chinese gambling game based on dream symbols. The night before Aunty Julie died of a heart attack my mother had a dream about her death.

No matter where we lived, it was important to Ma that we were well dressed, and she bought us good-quality clothes and shoes. On our birthdays, at Deepawali (the festival of lights), and at Christmas she would take us to Woolworths in West Street. In my adolescence, she sewed me fashionable clothes. Her foot moved quickly up and down on the pedal underneath the black Singer sewing machine with its beautiful gold writing. At 12 and 13 I got the beige and aubergine hot pants, miniskirt, halter neck and gillet that everyone was wearing. Ma bought me platform shoes and bell-bottomed, Crimplene pants. I had my hair cut in a short Twiggy style. School clothes, however, were often a size or two bigger to allow space for my growth spurts. Ma skimped on spending

money on herself and bought cheap clothes from discount stores. Still, even the cheapest dress looked like an expensive one from an upmarket store when she wore it. Years later Dad made Ma laugh at herself when he used a line in his play from one of their arguments, after she had admonished him for being wasteful while she used 'torn, torn panties'.

Aunty Julie was the mother of our friends Sophia, Banu, Fazilla, Naseema and Saleem. Though they were Muslim and we were Hindu, religious difference was not an obstacle to our close friendship. Muslim, Christian and Hindu tenants alike were united in dislike of our exploitative Muslim landlord. Yet we did not let his mean spirit stop us as we celebrated all the feasts. When it was Eid all of us ran together to check if the mosque light was on – the signal for the end of the fast – which we proclaimed in loud shouts: 'Lights on, lights on.' When it was Christmas, in Durban's subtropical heat, we ate turkey and had Christmas lunch, sang Christmas carols and exchanged presents around the Christmas tree. At our family altar there were symbols of other religions alongside our lamp. At Deepawali, our friends gathered around our clay lamps with the firecrackers which Dad had bought and Ma shared among us.

For Deepawali, Ma soaked and ground dhal, chillies and dhania, and spent ages rolling the mixture into a paste with a stone shaped like a rolling pin over a grinding stone. She shaped it into flat circles with a hole in the centre and fried them into tasty, crisp *vaddhas*. She sat painstakingly folding samoosas before frying them, and made rotis and sweetmeats like *polys* (coconut-filled pastries), *goolgoolas* (round balls of sweetened dough), and my favourite, *goolab jamun*, made from condensed milk and flour.

We woke early on Deepawali day and had our routine 'oil bath', with Ma pouring castor oil into our eyes, coconut oil on our heads and sweet oil into our ears before our bath. I hated the smell of castor oil; Ma gave us a tablespoonful to drink with an orange to

wash down the taste. At night we filled the clay lamps with oil and rolled cotton wool into wicks. We helped Ma place them outside on our windowsills before she lit them. All over Durban the lamps on windowsills lit up the darkness during the 'festival of lights'. When the inevitable thunderstorm broke, the rain steamed off hot tarred roads and the lamps were whisked indoors.

One of my most memorable and colourful Deepawalis began with a fight between my parents over the big box of fireworks that Dad had bought. Ma berated him for his extravagance throughout the drive to the beach. Once there, Dad placed the box on the bonnet of his car. Somehow a spark got into the box and resulted in a spectacular display of fireworks going off simultaneously in all directions. We were treated to a glorious cacophony of sound and kaleidoscope of colour that drowned out my mother's complaints.

Ma bought a cat to chase away the rats and mice, and it soon gave birth to a litter of kittens. She would put the basket of kittens outside while she cleaned the flat. One morning, I spotted a group of boys poking at the kittens with sticks and yelled for her. When she came outside, it was too late, the damage was done. The kittens had to be taken to the SPCA. My parents whispered so that I could not hear what they said to each other. I knew it meant the kittens would die so I surreptitiously hid the least injured one in my bed. I put a small stick on its injured leg and tied it straight. When Gus, my injured kitten, grew into a healthy cat, we took him with us on our annual trip to visit Dad's family in Cape Town. On our return journey, I nodded off to sleep. When I woke at a farm stall I called out for Gus, but there was no response and no sign of him anywhere.

Ma suggested that perhaps Gus had escaped when Dad stopped the car for Pat to pee. The toilets at the garages along the way were segregated into 'European' and 'Non-European'. The 'Non-European' toilets always seemed to be hidden at the back and were never cleaned, so Dad would stop along the road when we needed

to pee as it was pleasanter in the bushes. We left Pat and Daya to search the area around the farm stall while we drove back. I was hoarse from shouting through the open window. Then we saw a big cat lying dead on the road. It was not Gus but I cried as I called out even louder. It was getting late and we had to hurry back for Pat and Daya. We were in the Orange Free State. Indians were not allowed to stay overnight in that province without a permit, and Dad would never apply for one. As we drove back Dad tried to comfort me by telling me that Gus would eat well – he would enjoy the mice in the fields, grow fat and remain healthy as he ran after them. At the farm stall Pat and Daya were sitting on top of a large haystack waiting for us. Gus was not there. The Afrikaner farmer was sympathetic but we were not allowed to look any further. The law was the law and Dad had to get us out of the Orange Free State. He drove fast to beat the curfew.

Perhaps this is how I developed my love of driving long distances at high speed. In those years, my love for speed caused trouble. As Dad drove us down Sydenham Hill, the steep hill connecting Sparks Road to town, I urged him to go – 'Faster, Dad, faster!' – while Daya, Pat and I laughed in the back seat. Towards the bottom of the hill there was a natural bump in the road that felt like a miniature roller-coaster if you were travelling fast. As we neared it, Dad went faster only to be flagged down by a traffic cop and given a speeding fine. As we drove off, my mother turned to me, 'You see what you caused, now!' before she turned on my father. 'You have no sense, listening to children.' We all kept quiet, a little bit cowed. Fortunately my father was often able to charm my mother out of her moments of anger. In fact, sometimes she managed it herself. In an argument I recollect from childhood, Ma furiously challenged my father's opposition to physical beatings. She expostulated: 'You … you will spare the child and spoil the rod!' We collapsed laughing – and my mother's anger dissolved as she heard what she'd said.

Three

TEACHERS

In 1965 I entered school in great excitement, with a spring and a hop in my step. Spearman Road Primary School was right next door to our home. I was eager to join Daya, who had started school. As Daya's bright smile vanished round the corner of the school building on his way inside, I would race after him. It was against the law to go to school before you turned six and I was four years old. My enthusiasm persuaded my father, who had little respect for any of apartheid's laws, to forge my birth certificate. The principal, Mr George Thumbadoo, turned a blind eye, as he thought I was 'intelligent'. The teachers did not share his opinion, especially when they turned round from the blackboard to discover that I had wandered off yet again. To their irritation, they often found me in the school gardens playing among the flowers.

At Essendene Primary, the school we went to after Spearman Road, the red dust of the sand covered everything. It was hard on the white school uniform and socks my mother wanted kept clean. In the photos of me and my cousin Premilla, my socks always seemed to be falling down, my dress crooked, as I stood with my

tummy sticking out, my hair slightly untidy. Premilla had long hair tied tightly into two neat plaits. Her dress and socks always seemed properly in place.

In Standard 1, while we were living in the garage, Daya and I attended Springfield Model Primary School. I loved English and hated arithmetic. My arithmetic teacher complained to my parents that when I made mistakes I tried to rub them out – but not with an eraser. No, I spat on the paper and rubbed out the figures with my finger, making holes on the page. Ma and Dad were asked to come in to discuss their 'problem child'. I do not remember more than this – probably because my brother Daya made life so much fun that I forgot its difficulties.

At lunchtime I joined him in playing on the huge rocks in the school grounds. Those were the days when we still played most games together, kicking the ball, climbing trees, running and swimming. In a few years' time Daya's friends would scoff at the idea of a girl joining them and I would stay behind and play 'girls' games' with my friend Fazilla, plaiting grass, which we pretended was our daughter's hair.

One day, en route to Springfield from Joosab's, one of the adult passengers pushed against me, causing me to fall off the packed bus. I rolled under it, bruised but safe. I was shocked at being shoved so roughly. Yet, this was mild compared with the spiteful episode that followed, when I arrived for my first day at St Anthony's Catholic School in my old green and white Springfield uniform. The first term of Standard 3 had already started and I had just turned nine years old. Two girls pulled my hair, kicked me under the desk and told me to go back to my old school. As their desk was behind me, they could easily poke, pull and pinch me, out of sight of the teacher. 'Don't you know our school uniform? What is this stupid green and white dress? Go back to where you came from,' they taunted.

From my first year at St Anthony's, I stammered and stuttered when I stood up to answer my class teacher. 'Talk clearly, girl.

Speak up, I can't hear you,' she would shout. My stammer became worse. In the lunch break I stood alone and watched horrified as a baby bird fell out of its nest and was poked at by children with sticks. I did not open my mouth. At night I dreamt of tying up my teacher in the sari she sometimes wore. I woke feeling guilty, worried that others would see what a bad girl I was.

My father's uncle, my favourite Chimama, came one day to fetch me from school. He was wearing his fisherman's hat, a comfortable pair of old pants, and weathered shoes. My classmate Veena saw him and laughed. 'Who is *that*?' she asked. 'Is he your gardener?' I mumbled agreement as I looked down and walked quickly towards him. I hated myself. I was a coward. I loved Chimama. He drove huge, heavy trucks all over the Transkei and we wrote to each other. He told me all kinds of things I would not have learnt about otherwise. 'I don't have much school education, only Standard 2. But I'm a student of life,' he wrote proudly in one of his letters.

At the end of every week in St Anthony's, all the classes proceeded in neat lines to the church at the bottom of the school grounds. I fell in line and tried to listen and follow the instructions carefully. It was my first time at the school church service. The church was huge and the roof felt very, very high above my head. In the windows were paintings through which the light filtered in different colours. A call was made for people to come forward to take communion. I watched the girls go up row by row and obediently joined in. I was quite far down the aisle, fascinated by and eagerly awaiting the paper-thin wafer that each child was receiving in the mouth from the priest's hand. Suddenly a voice summoned me loudly. 'Get back to your seat, Pregaluxmi. This is for Catholic girls only.' The voice belonged to the teacher who lived next door to us in Joosab's Building and knew all our family secrets. I scuttled back to my seat, mortified and too embarrassed to look anywhere but at my brown Bata shoes.

The girls of St Anthony's oozed confidence. They didn't just do ballet, which I quickly gave up after feeling like an elephant amongst swans. They did speech and drama and shaved their legs. There were a few outsiders and I took to them. Arthi Ramkisson was intelligent, boyish, and had unshaved, unlotioned legs that the other girls giggled about. I liked her devil-may-care attitude. The Thomas sisters, Beverley Anne (Bev) and Juanita Rose (Junie), were also on the margins. They lived in a block of flats in Overport also owned by our landlord, Joosab. Their advantage was that they were Christian and their mother, Aunty Mary, was the popular Standard 1 teacher whom all the children adored. Bev, whom I quickly grew to love, was calm and centred, the original warm, friendly girl next door, though I identified more with Junie's slightly manic intelligence and humour, which I enjoyed fully when we became close friends at university. Pearl Choonoo lived in Himalaya Flats in Warwick Avenue Triangle, and in matric she became my best friend. Pearl had a quick and quirky intelligence and we giggled as we shared NikNaks under our desk lids and rewrote a bawdier version of our matric set works, *Vanity Fair* and Shakespeare.

On my first day in Standard 3, I met Alison (Alley) Lazarus, the class monitor. The teacher who showed me to my class smiled at a short, pretty girl with neat, tight plaits. 'Alison will take care of you.' The girl smiled back confidently at the teacher and nodded her head. Alison was the leader of the popular group in class. She often had tea at her home in Villa Road. The first time I was invited, I sat in awe. Her house looked like the home of Dad's white boss at the brewery. The first and only time we visited him, I had spilt tea on the carpet. I was terrified I would do the same in the house in Villa Road. The other girls, including the two who had tormented me on my first day, looked completely at ease. They discussed an ice-show, assuming that everyone attended them. I did not mention that my father received, and then tore up,

complimentary invitations from the white-run, racially segregated theatres. Most middle-class Indians saw nothing wrong in attending segregated shows, and boycotts were far from the norm.

I returned from Alison's tea, upset with my father. Why could we not see these shows, too? I wanted to be part of the popular group. He did not patronise me. Instead he explained that to accept going to a segregated show was to accept being seen as inferior. He refused to let his plays be performed at segregated venues or for the national broadcaster, the SABC. He criticised Indians hankering after acceptance by white society, giving me the example of Indians who garlanded white people and fed them breyani and samoosas, even the apartheid State President. He challenged me: 'Why should Indians identify with white South Africans who call themselves Europeans and not Africans? Africa is our home.' I did not really want to see the ice-show, I just wanted to belong to the group, but I could not explain this to my father. It would be years before I expressed my observation that he didn't draw the line at the segregated pubs which he enjoyed.

As a child, I loved all the things my father did with us: the spontaneous Sunday morning trips to the beach, the dancing at the Green Cat where he compèred shows, the soccer matches where he was commentator, the wonderful discussions about everything in life, his plays that made people laugh and think. At the Green Cat, Dad, Ma, Daya and I would dance around the room as Pat wove in and out between our legs. We had lots of fun together as a family. I grew up wanting to be like my father, whom everyone seemed to know and to like. I did not register the critical difference between us: he was a man in a man's world. He had the choices that men everywhere seemed to have. He escaped the drudgery of the essential, everyday cleaning and ironing, of cooking and raising children in Durban's humidity. Like most other men, he had the choice of leaving these chores to his wife while he could be politically active, socialise and have fun. Men were

engaged in the powerful work of making and changing the world – a world which excluded childcare, cleaning and cooking. In that world, boys were expected to 'sow their wild oats'. In contrast, girls were expected to be virgins who would grow into faithful wives. Girls and women who broke the social codes courted disgrace for themselves and their families. In this world, my father's affair was no big deal. For me, it felt as if the world was tumbling down.

In the privacy of the bathroom, I forgot my parents' fights. Although I was excruciatingly shy, once I closed the bathroom door I transformed into a glamorous singer. My voice would soar into loud, uninhibited song while I danced around the small space. Immersed in pouring the water from our bucket bath over myself one day, I looked up and saw a teenage boy who was visiting Joosab's Building peering through the window, which he had managed to open. I screamed and my mother came running in. She raced out and found the culprit, for whom life as a peeping tom was hopefully cut short.

The year I stopped stammering in school was the year I created my charcoal drawing. One day in Standard 5 our art teacher, Mr Nanackchand, told us to use whatever medium we wanted. He had a wide selection for us – crayons, pastels, paint and charcoal. Everyone rushed for the crayons and pastels. I am not sure if I picked up the stick of charcoal because I wanted to or because I was the last to reach his desk. The coal made my fingers black. I drew a face, the face of a man. A beard. Eyes in dark and light, coal against white. I smudged lines around them and on his forehead. This was so much fun. The teacher's voice broke through: 'I'm coming round now to look at your work. It's time to select the piece for the school display cabinet.' I looked up and looked around. Clean white sheets with homes, gardens and people in bright pastel shades of pink, yellow, green, red and blue. Panic, shame. Hide the drawing, squash it into my desk, tuck my hands away.

He was behind me, then next to me. 'Where's your drawing?' Silence. 'You were busy. Take it out. I want to see what you drew.' I took it out, straightened up the mess, and waited to hear the insults and shouting. He was going to see what a disgraceful girl I was. Everyone was going to see my dirty black hands. All the children with their neat, pretty drawings were going to laugh even more. The girls in the popular group would whisper and make it clear that I was not welcome. I hated school. I wished I never needed to come back. The teacher picked up my drawing and was silent for a long time. I heard him saying wonderful things and looked up from my shoes and smudged fingers. For the next week each time we filed past, I stole glances at the school display cabinet. My heart filled up and floated right past the church steeple.

The year after my charcoal drawing I was in the class of my favourite teacher in St Anthony's, Mrs Nair. Mrs Nair's homely sari and her old-fashioned spectacles belied her razor-sharp mind. With her kind heart she inspired me to produce my best school results that year. At the end of Standard 6, Alley Lazarus (our class monitor in Standard 3) and I became close friends. She confided that her parents were going through a divorce and she shared her fear that the Catholic Church would excommunicate her family as divorce was forbidden. She visited me in our flat in Joosab's Building and got to know my brother Daya. They began dating about a year later.

Most of my friends were dating by this stage and I was the odd one out. The end of my stammer did not signal the end of my shyness, particularly with boys, in whose company I froze. The boys in my Standard 6 class called me Madame Curie not just because I loved science but because of my unapproachable façade. Yet I had an erotic imagination, which I fed with all the books I could get my hands on. I dwelt on the love scenes in D.H. Lawrence, adored the erotica of *The Arabian Nights* and the bawdy passages in our Shakespeare and Chaucer set works. I had an active fantasy life.

In these years, I saw Sydney Poitier in *To Sir, with Love* and Omar Sharif in *Dr Zhivago* and fell in love with both of them.

Uma, Gandhi's granddaughter, was head prefect at St Anthony's. She led an anti-Republic Day campaign at the school and Daya, who was in Standard 6, was actively involved. I cannot remember more than the anti-Republic Day slogans on the walls. The protest registered itself in my memory as support for my brother's stand.

By Standard 7, however, I was no longer just supporting my brother's political activities. I was developing my own independent views. When an Irish nun asked us to stand up and sing 'Die Stem', the national anthem of apartheid South Africa, I remained seated. I kicked the chair of the girl in front of me: 'Sit down. Pass it on.' She stopped singing 'Die Stem', sat down, and kicked the chair of the girl in front of her. After class, the nun summoned me to her room. She seemed genuinely perplexed and we ended up having the first of many discussions about South Africa. We talked about everything, from apartheid to the gangsters and prostitutes in Sparks Road.

At home Daya taught me Marx's famous saying, 'Religion is the opiate of the masses', and I read his copy of the Bhagavad Gita. Its image of war disturbed me. I wished that another image had been used to convey its message that the greatest battle is not for sovereignty over others but over ourselves. I also wanted to challenge the belief in God. Where was this God when good people suffered? I wanted to discuss my concerns with the learned people of the ashram, whose yoga class I attended. I collected and read the ashram's literature on Hinduism and questioned the swami about the caste system and the roles given to men and women. Celibacy was upheld in their texts as the only route to enlightenment and women were referred to as sources of the 'temptation of lust' that young men must avoid 'till they become householders and marry'. Even Gandhi perpetuated this stereotype. In his 'experiments with truth' he tested his commitment to sexual

abstinence by sleeping next to young virgin girls. His self-imposed tests affirmed his celibacy as well as society's prejudice that women are objects to satiate or test men's desire. Sex was the great taboo. The ashram's books did not deal with the *Kama Sutra*, where sex was celebrated.

The swami was not very amenable to debate and was focused instead on the work of the ashram. They did valuable work including building desks and chairs for African schools. African schools were completely under-resourced – at the time government spent less than R100 on the education of each African child while it spent well over a R1000 on a white child. I felt guilty that my concerns were a frivolous distraction. Daughters, wives and women yogis were expected to be of a sweet and pleasing temperament, not discontented and argumentative. But the question of selflessness in religion and politics perplexed me. I saw that many of those preaching selflessness were inflated, pompous people who believed they were the voice of God or of the revolution. Yet selflessness inspired me. A quote I put up in every office I occupied as an adult read, 'Of the best leaders, when their work is done the people will say, "We have done it ourselves."'

A *Swami* was the title of one of my favourite plays written by my father. The swami had fallen from grace and was abandoned by all those who had hailed him before. I cried when I watched the swami, played by Dad's handsome cousin Kessie. I watched Dad teach Kessie the craft of theatre, when he came to our flat after a hard day's work as a builder. In Dad's play the swami wept, wildly searching for our most primal connection: 'Mother, Mother, where are you? I need you, Mother, do not leave me.' Kessie had a beautiful voice and as swami he sang a haunting melody about the goddess as creator and destroyer. I was moved, too, by my father's generosity. His plays were popular, yet he allowed me to correct his words, treating my changes with respect.

In early adolescence I began consciously to distance myself

from my father, not wanting to be known as 'Ronnie's daughter'. Despite my closeness to him, I grew highly critical. Newly aware of his contradictions, I wasted little time in pointing them out to him, with none of the patience or tolerance he showed towards me. I wanted him to be the disciplined, wise elder who had found and was living the truth; the yogi who renounced alcohol, meat and all 'vices'; a faithful husband who was beyond reproach; a role model. Today in his seventies, my father, still writing life, is as ready for a good party as he ever was. He still has the green fingers that create wild and wonderful gardens out of barrenness, and claims that his daily tots of whisky are medicinal.

By Standard 7 in St Anthony's, my instinctive resistance to the school was deepened by the attitude of the Indian teachers who seemed more European than the white nuns. This was the ethos we were being groomed into, and I slowly, firmly began to dig in my heels. I poured my creative energy into writing my first 'political' speech about apartheid, which I delivered in class. Our Indian teacher, who ironically carried the Afrikaner name of one of the regime's presidents, said in a clipped English accent, 'Do not ask your father to write your speeches for you.' I walked back to my desk in silence. My father had not read my speech, had not contributed one word to it. Her insult cut deeper than the wild slapping of my Afrikaans teacher the year before, who had had to be stopped by the boys in the class when I refused to cry.

After Standard 7 I attended Durban Indian Girls' High. It was 1974, and I resolved not to please anyone but myself in what I wrote and said. I learnt later of Steve Biko's book, *I Write What I Like*. In class I wrote and said things that should have shocked Mrs Royeppen. The neat twinsets, pearls and Gatsby wave in her short hair were deceptive. She refused to be shocked even when I started a speech quoting Wally Serote's poem entitled 'What's in This Black "Shit"' or wrote a book review of Xaviera Hollander's biography of her life as a prostitute.

In high school I learnt about the racism of Harper Lee's America in *To Kill a Mockingbird*, the child labour of Charles Dickens's industrial capitalism, George Orwell's attack on totalitarianism in *Animal Farm*, and the anti-Semitism that provoked Shylock's speech in *The Merchant of Venice*. For me, these writers exposed the totalitarianism of the apartheid state, the exploitation of capitalism and the ugliness of racism. My love for literature inspired my politics despite a syllabus limited to European and American writers.

In 1974, Portuguese colonialism was overcome in neighbouring Mozambique. Daya took me to the rally at Curries Fountain to celebrate Frelimo's victory. He held my hand tight as we ran from the soldiers who broke up the rally. The organisers would end up jailed on Robben Island for many years. I read Samora Machel's speech on the emancipation of women and quoted his famous lines again and again: 'The liberation of women is a fundamental necessity for our revolution, a guarantee of its continuity and a precondition for victory.'

High school was an important learning ground. In my first year an older group of girls approached me. They explained that they planned to form a pupils' representative council (PRC), a first for the school. I was the youngest member elected onto the council and was appointed secretary. When I reached Standard 9 the PRC organised an interschool social with our 'brother' school, Sastri College. A Muslim organisation decided this would lead good Muslim girls astray and discussed it in the Grey Street mosque.

The fundamentalist leader of the mosque was fanatically opposed to other religions. He issued inflammatory pamphlets about Hindus, Jews and Christians, in which he argued that there was no other God but Allah and that everyone else, especially Hindus, would burn in the fires of eternal hell. The mosque issued a public warning against our social, calling on all good Muslim girls to boycott it and their families to act against it. They did not make

a similar call to the boys of Sastri College. Their announcement in the mosque appeared on the front pages of a local newspaper. We insisted on going ahead. Many Muslim girls ignored the call.

A short while after the social, Daya told me about an illegal fund for political detainees. I agreed to raise money for it and went from class to class asking pupils to collect money 'for a good cause', which I did not name. In the Standard 9 class the teacher stopped Farieda, a Muslim student, collecting money, and asked her what she was doing and who had asked her. Farieda was unable to say what the 'good cause' was because she didn't know. Farieda's teacher was a member of the Muslim organisation that had opposed the PRC social. She promptly reported me to the principal. I remembered how I had provoked this teacher's anger before: she had been present when I had addressed the class about the controversial social. With no subtlety at all, I'd told students to ignore the call from the mosque: 'Those who have evil in their hearts will see evil in innocence. Muslim girls, don't feel intimidated by bigots.'

The principal summoned me. I knew what lay in store. Her husband, who had once been a respected leader of the community, was now a member of the apartheid President's Council. As I walked to her office I sent a message to Alley via our 'live telegraph', a whispered message to a student seated at a window I passed: 'Tell Alison it's the milk fund.' In the office the principal demanded that I disclose the fund I had asked the girls to collect money for. I said it was the milk fund. She knew I was lying and threatened to report me to the Security Branch, apartheid's terrifying political police. She spoke darkly about my personal file, which the guidance teacher, Mrs Desai, was in charge of. My fear vanished because I knew that gentle, soft-spoken Mrs Desai would not support the principal. I persisted: 'The PRC was collecting money for the *Daily News* milk fund – it is a legal charity.' Fortunately, when Alley, then head girl, was summoned,

she backed my story. All the money collected was donated to the milk fund and not to the detainees.

In a debate with Gandhi Desai High School I encountered the boy who would become my first boyfriend and then husband, father of Parusha and Yashodan, and finally ex-husband. He was tall and wore glasses, which made him look intelligent. His hair was longer than the standard school length. The topic we debated was 'Women are the weaker sex' and Jayendra Naidoo's team argued for this position, fighting for the patriarchal mindset that dominated society. Our team, a group of serious young feminists who may or may not have heard the term 'feminist' at this stage of our lives, disputed the motion and won.

Mrs Royeppen decided to dramatise *An Inspector Calls*, a social commentary on class in industrial England. She chose me to play the role of the inspector and Alley to play the daughter of the factory owner. In every rehearsal I collapsed in mirth, being set off by Mano, the actress playing the factory owner, whose laughter could be detected in an expansive shaking tummy and bright eyes. Mrs Royeppen was panicking by the time of the first performance, as up to that point hysteria had made me forget most of my lines. In the actual performance we all remembered our parts. A girl in our class wrote in the school magazine that we had all 'enlightened the audience as much about each character's particular vision as of the play itself'. In the post-show photos there is one of my friend Saguna Gordhan (Sags) with me in my inspector's suit and moustache. We hold each other, laughing, her laugh rippling from dimpled cheeks to eyes.

The principal's husband invited his friend Lucas Mangope, who headed the bantustan of Bophuthatswana, to the opening of the play. Sags's uncle Pravin Gordhan also attended. But it was the tin-pot homeland leader who was brought to shake our hands, not this activist who had begun to help organise the 'Indian community' in Durban against the apartheid state.

Government schools were divided strictly along racial and ethnic lines and our PRC decided we should meet with students from other 'races'. We planned to meet our contemporaries from Inanda Seminary, a school for African girls. Instead, our principal decided that we had to meet pupils from Michaelhouse, an exclusive boarding school for white boys. Our resistance to her suggestion was defeated by her argument that if we wanted to be nonracial, as we claimed, we had to meet with them first. Fortunately, the boys of Michaelhouse did not match my neat stereotypes. One of the boys I spoke to was reading the hefty tomes of Karl Marx's *Das Kapital* in his research for a school history project, while I had read only a very slim *Communist Manifesto*, which I treated as an act of great secrecy and subversion. Our conversation quickly pushed me off my high horse.

Two essays that I wrote in the matric trial exams appeared in the school magazine. The English one, 'Shoddy philosophies', was praised by the principal's husband, oblivious of the fact that the essay was inspired by criticism of 'cultured Indians' like himself, who knew their ragas and served apartheid on the President's Council. It also condemned the war in Vietnam, specifically the massacre of innocent Vietnamese women and children in My-Lai. 'Someone said it was the essence and not the appearance which mattered ... Jesus Christ wore his hair long but Sergeant Daly, the all-American soldier who mercilessly shot down women and children, had a crew-cut antiseptic appearance.'

The Afrikaans essay, 'Eenheid, rustigheid en skoonheid' (Unity, peacefulness and purity), criticised the mining magnate Harry Oppenheimer for his materialism. Following this, my Afrikaans teacher asked me to write an essay celebrating the 1976 centenary of the Afrikaans language. I liked my Afrikaans teacher but would not let my words celebrate this event while students younger than me, like Hector Pieterson, were being killed for protesting against Afrikaans in Soweto. I refused to write the essay.

In 1976, the principal invited one of the leaders of the Liberal Party, the author Alan Paton, as guest speaker. At the time, Paton had been defending Gatsha Buthelezi, even though Buthelezi's Inkatha Freedom Party seemed to us a willing collaborator with the apartheid government in its attacks against young students in Natal's townships. A few of us walked out as Paton began his speech. The year 1976 was also when all the prefects, in a demonstration of united resistance, handed in their badges.

I was a rebellious teenager in apartheid South Africa. On a warm summer evening that year, as my mother and I walked along the beach to buy ice creams, some white youths whistled and catcalled at me. I ignored them and they shouted out, 'Go back to India, coolie bitch' and other obscenities. My mother was anxious as I turned round and challenged them: 'You bastards, who do you think you're talking to?' 'Just walk on,' my mother whispered under her breath. 'You never know what they could do to you.' She was angry with me; she knew what they did to you. But I refused to accept that I belonged elsewhere, not in my country or on my continent.

My mother feared that politics would interrupt my education and get me into trouble. At home she would leave my brothers and father alone when yet another debate started up. I, on the other hand, was ordered to follow a role I strenuously resisted: 'Come to the kitchen and grate the carrots, now!' We had a difficult relationship. Ma wanted me to be a teacher, like her, and hoped I would have a stable life. She did not want any of her children to experience the poverty she had been through. A university education, a steady job, marriage and children were her dreams for each of us.

As I reflect on life's lessons in writing this book, it dawns on me for the first time that my children Parusha and Yashodan share exactly the same age difference as my older brother Daya and I. My mother and I were the same age when we gave birth to our first

two children. Like me and like my daughter, my mother was her mother's only daughter. Like my mother, I love teaching. Deeply embedded in my DNA, the pattern of my mother, Kamalam the lotus flower, danced fiercely as it weaved her design into my life despite my conscious resistance.

STUDENT LIFE

Daya attended the University of Natal's Medical School, where Steve Biko had been a student. He would come home and talk to me about Biko and Black Consciousness. As part of his course, Daya had to dissect cadavers – dead bodies of human beings. He hated this part of the course. In apartheid South Africa all the bodies the students cut were black people who were too poor for proper funerals.

One day he came home very angry that the army had broken up a demonstration he had been part of, with mainly African students. He was upset that many of the Indian students, who generally stuck to themselves, did not join the protest. Biko's Black Consciousness appealed to me and I readily accepted and identified myself as black. I had always hated the way we were labelled 'non-European' or 'non-white' – all in the negative, not something positive. We lived and grew up in racial and ethnic division – 'Indian', 'Coloured', 'African' or 'white' areas, beaches, schools, universities. Even in writing this book, I find it impossible to write about South Africa in this period without using these racial terms, despite believing that we are a single human race.

In those early years, political ideas were not the only ones that Daya introduced me to. One of the books he showed me was *Straight and Crooked Thinking*, which helped me to spot dishonest arguments and made me aware when I myself was using them. Daya's passion was physics. He linked physics and ideas he had learnt from the Bhagavad Gita, fascinated that a part of us is limited by time and space while another infinitesimal part is eternal energy. Daya had a spiritual strength – the mantra he meditated on throughout his life meant 'God is love, love is God'. Daya kept his faith in love. He married Alley, his childhood sweetheart, in 1980 and they named their three children Karlind (sun), Triya (female) and Disha (guidance and direction).

In high school and university Daya shared with me the things that captivated him: the fluidity of energy which is life, the impact of the theories of Newton and Einstein on people's view of themselves and the world, and the way static science had given way to the theory of relativity. He tried to make me understand its implications for the future. We talked about justice, famine and inequality as we listened to his record of *The Concert for Bangladesh*. Daya's records included a version of *The Prophet* by Khalil Gibran, sung by Richard Harris: 'Your children are not your children ... they are life's longing for itself.'

It wasn't all serious stuff. Our new home in middle-class Reservoir Hills was surrounded by garden on all sides except the front, which was the driveway. One of our jobs was to clear the garden of endless rocks and stones, to make way for the indigenous trees, flowers and fruit that Dad planted. One day, while sitting on a rock in shorts with my legs sprawled out, digging out stones, I uncovered a nest of snakes. In Daya's hilarious version, the snakes gave me the power of flight as I leapt up and ran to him on the veranda, breathless and utterly incoherent.

At the University of Durban-Westville (UDW) I enrolled for an engineering degree. The student counsellor's advice was

that engineering would combine my love for the creativity I'd experienced in English and the science of physics, my two best matric subjects. But as I struggled with technical drawing, I realised I wouldn't catch up with the other students, all except one of them boys who had studied the subject throughout high school.

Before the year was out I was given a chance to study journalism, which was what I really wanted to do. My father nurtured my interest in it. Three of his brothers were journalists; the eldest became a successful writer, particularly with a book on Patrice Lumumba, the first democratically elected prime minister of the Congo. I learnt that the Americans, British, Belgians and South Africans had jointly conspired to murder Lumumba, a man of vision, values and principled commitment to the poor. In his place they installed Mobutu, a man of greed who protected their mining interests. The story inspired me: I wanted to learn how to investigate and expose the facts, instead of the propaganda that the SABC fed us.

In my mother's arguments about the unreliability of journalists, she didn't refer to the married, conventionally reputable writer, but to the two other brothers, who travelled around without 'stability', and didn't marry either. She ranked them alongside my father's journalist friends as a dissolute, 'drunken bunch of men'. She was adamant that I should not go down that road, which was 'too unstable for a woman'. Her view won out, but I rebelled against her as I dropped out of the engineering degree and took up part-time work doing market research. She was busy working all day and didn't know the risks I took in my free time. Alone, I explored Durban's beaches north and south on the train that runs alongside them. The sea, which I had fallen in love with in childhood, sustained me in adolescence as my rebellious anger slowly faded. It was a sweet irony that years later, as an adult woman in my forties, I was awarded, and accepted, a fellowship from a graduate school of journalism.

In 1977 I began studying towards a BA degree with English and history majors, psychology, philosophy and a non-degree course in art. On the first day the white art lecturer, in hippie clothing and sandals, asked us to introduce ourselves. Midway she stopped us, exasperated. 'Don't you people have shorter names?' The introductions began again, this time with everyone using 'Christian' or European names. When it was my turn, I said I was Pregaluxmi Govender. 'Don't you have a shorter name?' she asked. 'No,' I insisted, 'my name is Pregaluxmi Govender.' At the end of the year she had forgotten most of the names except the longest one.

Throughout my university days I supplemented my history lectures with intense study groups, and learnt lessons from other countries. I read about political struggles in the rest of Africa, in South America, Russia, Cuba, China, India and Europe, and made connections between historical and contemporary protest. In literature I loved Sembene Ousmane's *God's Bits of Wood* for its sharp, nuanced depiction of working-class reality. Chinua Achebe's *A Man of the People* issued timely warnings of what we should not become: a postcolonial elite out to get rich as quickly as possible, with no qualms about emulating one's past masters. From writers like Virginia Woolf and James Joyce I caught a playfulness with words. Through adolescence to adulthood, writing remained a habit of recording the detail of experience as well as a creative way of coping with complexity.

In my sociology class, I met my debating opponent from high school, Jayendra. We talked about Marx, Engels, Lenin and Gramsci while we worked together in communities around Durban and began dating. My closest friends and family did not like him; I insisted that they did not know him as I did. I met his mother, Sanna, who laughed a lot despite struggling against the conservatism which dictated that good Indian wives had to be subordinate to their husbands and could not be independent and

creative. I introduced Sanna to my friends and comrades, who loved her, and she revelled in their young company. When Sanna's art was eventually published by *Speak* magazine, I kidnapped her in her nightgown for celebratory ice creams on Durban's beachfront. 'What will people say?' she giggled, savouring ice cream and freedom in her nightgown as we laughed our way down West Street, holding hands.

In the final year of my degree, students across South Africa joined a boycott that was initiated by students who were still at school. During the boycott a core group of political activists from Durban, of which I was part, met almost every night to plan and strategise. We knew each other well from working together in mainly 'Indian' townships in community structures set up by the NIC (Natal Indian Congress), a political organisation that was an ally of the African National Congress. The NIC, which had been formed in 1894, had had leaders of the calibre of Monty Naicker and George Sewpersadh, who had fought apartheid all their lives.

In 1980, our group met with students from across the country, translating theory into practical strategies. When the massive student body congregated in the open air or in halls, we sang and danced as we chanted freedom songs. Student musicians like Shireen Bickram, our own Joan Baez, sang the songs of Bob Dylan, Pete Seeger and Baez, too.

We organised a rally together with students from other universities, technikons and high schools and spread out across Durban mobilising school students to board buses headed for UDW. I went to my old high school, Durban Indian Girls' High, wearing the school blazer. The girls worked well together and were soon on a bus. My old school principal looked disconcerted as she spotted me disappearing round a school wall. The army was everywhere and many buses were stopped before reaching UDW.

We arrived safely but were blocked from entering the campus by soldiers at the entrance.

Instead of vacating the campus as we were ordered, many of us barricaded ourselves into the women's hostel. There was pure glee on the faces of my friends Rajni Manga and Vishu Lakhoo as we poured washing powder onto the floor in front of the locked doors and aimed fire hosepipes, ready to turn the area into a slippery nightmare for the soldiers. Upstairs on the roof several of us took another hosepipe and aimed it at the dogs, preparing to hose them down if they came too close to the hostel. We were serious young women, laughing as we learnt to defend ourselves against the soldiers.

Quite early in our boycott, the army charged at us with batons, tear gas and dogs. I had seen how young and fit the soldiers looked – but I wore tackies, had long legs, and could run fast. When they attacked I sprinted to the top of a hill and then watched outraged as soldiers obscenely relished attacking those who could not run as fast because of high heels or because they were pregnant. As their batons connected, they swore at the women and called them bitches and whores. There was a weird comic scene when one of the male students hopped while taunting the soldier whose baton kept bouncing off his head. His defiant laughter belied the pain the baton must have caused. My Afrikaner history lecturer, who had been furious when I challenged his statement about the existence of pure races, stood with the security forces, wearing a tear-gas mask.

Alley, heavily pregnant, stood with me watching the soldiers' brutality from a safe vantage point. There were other pregnant women who were being caught. I proposed that we go to the highest authority, to the rector's office, and stop this outrage. We had no clearer plan than that. Sags, who was with us, had written in her matric farewell message to me: 'I promise I'll be there, comrade.' Sure enough, on that day in 1980, Sags was there with her own car, and she drove us to the rector.

We realised we would never get through the front entrance,

which was heavily guarded by soldiers, so we walked round to the back, where soldiers were letting in members of Council, who were mostly white with a few Indian lackeys. We pushed through them. The rector, rumoured to be a member of the Broederbond, the all-powerful Afrikaner secret society, was in their midst. I shouted at him that the soldiers were tear-gassing and beating his students. 'You are the rector of this university. You are responsible. They are tear-gassing even pregnant students. If anything happens to Alison or her baby, we will hold you personally responsible. Stop them now.' He looked embarrassed and avoided my eyes as he tried steering us into his office. 'Miss Govender, please let's talk about this. Come, come into my office.' We wanted him to use his power to get the soldiers off the campus. He wanted me to sit in his office as we had done the year before when I was part of the team negotiating a democratic SRC. He wanted us to talk as if nothing were happening outside his door. Sags, Alley and I walked out in anger and disgust.

The following day large numbers of us reconvened on the campus even though we had been ordered not to. We sat singing defiantly in the square between the library and the cafeteria. The security forces announced their countdown before attacking with dogs and batons. We scattered. A few of us ran in the direction of the engineering faculty buildings, picked up some of the sticks and metal pipes lying around, and ran directly back at the men in uniform. It was a moment of madness I'll never forget. Our sticks and pipes were useless against guns, batons and dogs, but logic did not stop us. And then something strange happened. The soldiers started backing away, fear in their eyes. Behind us a momentum grew and the victory washed away my fear of men with guns.

I wish this chapter could end with this demonstration of unity, of clear-cut 'good against evil' and without any grey areas of

confusion or doubt. In that moment we seemed to share clarity about who and what we were fighting and a belief that we ourselves would never abuse power like apartheid's rulers. It was a simplistic assumption that because we were fighting the evil of apartheid and belonged to the same broad movement, we shared the same values and understanding of power and leadership. In fact the struggle against apartheid was not a neatly unified one. It was often bitterly divided, not to mention the divisions created by the Inkatha Freedom Party, which was funded by the state and operated as a vicious agent of apartheid.

There were many examples of such division. I remember being part of a group of young NIC activists who broke up a meeting that was being addressed by Saths Cooper, a leader of the Black Consciousness Movement. Outside Sath's meeting, intellectual engagement gave way to thuggery as shouting and labelling almost degenerated into fisticuffs. I recall shifting within myself from hurling insults to feeling a sense of shame at my own behaviour. It was easy to behave as an unthinking idiot, part of the popular group ganging up against one person.

In Natal a major division developed within our movement, between those who were within and those who were against the 'cabal', a small group of older, mostly NIC comrades who regarded themselves, and who were recognised, as the internal voice of the ANC. Critics of the cabal did not have an easy time and were often labelled 'ultra-leftists', 'individualists' and 'workerists' (referring to those who believed that trade unions should only address workplace issues rather than political ones or those facing workers in their communities). Few of us who were given such labels over the years subscribed to such narrow beliefs or practices. However, once identified and labelled, we were excluded from structures linked to the NIC, as leaders of the cabal were the gatekeepers of activists from the 'Indian community' into the leadership and sometimes even membership of the ANC in exile or the United

Democratic Front (UDF), the powerful mass movement which was formed in 1983 to unite opposition to apartheid.

A few years later, when I returned to UDW as a postgraduate student and teacher in the English Department, I was elected to chair the labour committee of the Community Services Unit (CSU). The CSU organised workers on the campus, who had to eat and change in the toilets and were paid very low wages. We used a simple questionnaire on which workers listed their grievances and their proposals for what action needed to be taken to resolve them, laying the basis for unionisation. In 1985, the year Cosatu was formed, the CSU organised a focus debate and invited several trade unionists to it, including Alec Erwin and Bobby Marie. They met with a flurry of opposition from the floor. Much of it came from the important men (all middle class and Indian) from the cabal who attended and who aggressively led the questioning of the speakers. UDW, an ethnic 'Indian' institution, was their territory and Cosatu, a non-racial trade union federation, was not warmly welcomed.

While I learnt a great deal from leaders of the cabal during my first student years while going from house to house with community campaigns in the 'Indian' townships, I became increasingly critical. The cabal's leaders were excellent in their ability to strategise and plan, but the desire to control everything and everyone was a huge weakness. Unless an initiative was controlled by the cabal, its members would try to destroy it, as they did with the Youth Forum. The Youth Forum had been helping youth organisations in Natal to educate and organise themselves in the fight against apartheid. A handful of individuals linked to the cabal felt their power base was being threatened and used their influence in the UDF to destroy this organisation. At a Youth Forum meeting in the Diakonia building, tempers flared as some people burned the Youth Forum's flag and talked of 'necklacing'.

'Necklacing' was horrific. In one of the first incidents the

state-run television showed a young woman, accused of being an 'impimpi' or informer, being held down, a tyre thrust over her and doused with petrol before being set alight. The camera did not shift its gaze as she was burnt alive. It later emerged that she was not an informer but was completely innocent. Necklacing was another weapon in the hands of those who wanted to punish or get rid of opponents and the apartheid state was quick to adopt it and include it in its bag of dirty tricks.

During the turbulent Youth Forum meeting at Diakonia, a woman I had known since our days together as students at UDW loudly announced to some youth attending the meeting that 'there are some in the UDF who are anti-UDF, like Pregs and Kumi'. Kumi Naidoo was attending the Forum as a youth activist, from the sprawling Indian working-class township of Chatsworth. I was present at the AGM of the Natal Organisation of Women (NOW), which was also being held in the Diakonia building. Unaware of her allegations, I walked about with my name tag prominently displayed. Jean Manning, one of NOW's older leaders, argued strongly that the organisation should take disciplinary action against the woman. Jean warned of the dangers of such labelling, reminding people that in a time of 'necklacing', such reckless allegations could precipitate an attack from someone who did not know me.

I am sure that this young woman and others like her did not appreciate the full consequences of destructive labels or the intangible viciousness of whispering campaigns, social ostracism and lost reputations. Kumi and I were luckier than those who did not have any struggle, family or class credentials to protect them against being labelled state informers. They faced the possibility of terrible retaliation from people who had suffered because of real informers. In the 1980s this became a widespread way of dealing with opposition within the country and in exile, by those who lacked personal and political maturity. Some comrades,

for example, were tortured in ANC camps after they had enthusiastically left the country hoping to serve the movement. Others were necklaced in townships.

During this complex time in our country, criticisms of the cabal became more pronounced: of its centralised and undemocratic manner of decision-making, its lack of respect for working-class leadership, the ethnic lines on which it organised, the chauvinism and sexist attitudes, its control of resources and the patronage of areas and individuals who were loyal, mainly in Indian, Coloured and very few African group areas. There were some in the NIC who said that they were anti-cabal yet, with few exceptions, many replicated these same patterns when they took positions as leaders. Later on, changes occurred in the leadership of the cabal, but this was not accompanied by any fundamental critique or alternative model of power and leadership.

When Mandela was released in 1990 and the exiles returned, those schooled in this narrow tradition of politics, whether inside or outside the country, continued to use their access to power to exclude others. In these years my best teachers included people I was critical of. I learnt crucial political lessons from them as from others. But, as I tried to pinpoint what it was I opposed in their practice, I was inspired to develop an alternative understanding and practice of power and leadership.

Five

THE PERSONAL IS POLITICAL

I was married in a traditional marriage in the Cato Manor temple, after a formal courtroom registration. I disliked a lot of the ceremony – the *thali* that Jayendra tied around my neck like a noose while the priest herded his mother Sanna and all her sisters behind me; the fact that my new husband had to step on my foot to symbolise the hierarchy of a good Telugu marriage; the coconut that I was told was symbolic of the bride's virginity – only the bride was expected to be virginal, not the groom. Perhaps the only thing I did like was the simple R60 ring the jeweller crafted to my design in place of the customary expensive jewellery which to me symbolised the bride being bought. Recently I visited an exhibition of Omar Badsha's work and stood in front of a photo entitled 'Hindu bride at wedding'. I did not immediately recognise myself as the skinny young woman standing next to the Hindu priest in a temple, wearing a sari and holding a coconut.

I was convinced that the baby growing inside me was a girl and made a collage with the photograph of a baby in the red glow of a womb and the words of Stevie Wonder: 'Isn't she lovely, isn't she

wonderful, isn't she precious!' Inside me I felt a gentle reassuring presence growing into her self. Throughout the pregnancy with my firstborn I walked to the market, which was a short distance from Scala's, our flat in Warwick Avenue. I savoured the smell of freshly picked green herbs, the dhania and mint, the mounds of green chillies and pungent onions, the feel and colour of smooth-skinned purple brinjals, potatoes with sand still on them and red, juicy tomatoes. I wanted to be as healthy as possible on the small budget we had, so I bought fruit and vegetables, which I liked and could afford. I started my morning with yoga and savoured the moments when my baby started to move around, stretching my skin softly with her foot or hand as she reached out into the world.

On the day my waters burst I instinctively knew what it meant, although I was slightly hesitant because Jayendra and I had not yet reached this chapter in the book on pregnancy we had been reading. At the hospital, Jayendra was unceremoniously ushered out of the ward before the nurse roughly administered the standard Minora blade shave before the enema. I quickly discovered that the hospital toilet was not working.

For the doctor's convenience, women's legs were strung up onto two stirrups, like a cow at an abattoir. When the doctor arrived, I insisted that the least he could do was allow Jayendra back in. He was still equivocating when a painful contraction made me yell for my husband. Our daughter arrived in the world and announced herself, before the normal slap doctors gave to satisfy themselves that the baby was breathing. I held her while the doctor stitched the cut he had made. That night I slept exhausted and woke energised, in love with this baby that looked deep into my eyes. I was out of the hospital early the next morning. Her father, at first traumatised by witnessing the birthing process I had been through, was entranced with our firstborn.

After our baby's birth I took her to my parents' home, where

my mother placed our precious bundle on the ground and said a prayer asking for the blessing of the earth, wind, fire and water. It was also a prayer for harmony with all four directions: east, west, north and south. She placed a dot in the centre of her forehead – on the *budhi*, the divine intellect. The time of our baby's birth resonated with the sound *p*, determined by the position of the planets, according to the temple guru my parents consulted. I liked the idea of our child in harmony with the universe and chose the name Parusha – 'the flowing waters' of a river in India. Every day I discovered new meanings in her name, but the image of the depth and the flow of water remains the most appropriate.

Parusha, whose name I sometimes shortened to Parush, was born a few days before Christmas. At my parents' home she took in everyone and everything with her big, brown eyes. My father and Pat fell in love with this little baby, as they had fallen in love the year before with Karlind, Daya and Alley's son. To help me recover, Ma asked Dad to go to Cato Manor and find the herbs that helped soften painful milk-hardened breasts and eased the fever. My mother lit a fire and threw *samrani* (frankincense) on it to heal the bruised pathway between womb and world. Afterwards she held Parusha over the smoke to clear her chest, but my baby wailed and I snatched her back, rejecting the tradition for gentler ways. A few days afterwards, both families gathered in my parents' garden to plant a fruit tree to celebrate Parusha's arrival. We finished lunch with sweet rice filled with almonds, raisins and elachi, which my mother had cooked.

Early in the morning my father would come to our bedroom to take Parusha to my mother, and they laughed and talked to her in their bed. Parusha's energy seemed to calm and relax all of us around her. In the warmth of the day Dad would take Parusha into the garden and lay her down on the grass next to him before settling down to read his book. This support in the weeks after Parusha's birth helped a lot, but it was not long before Jayendra

and I took our new baby back to our own flat. Parush and then her brother Yashodan never tired of visiting my parents' garden. With their cousins Karlind, Triya, Disha and Kamil they would spin magic as they clambered through its trees and bushes.

◎

At that time I was working as a teacher, and Jayendra had a job at a bank before being offered a job in the trade union we had both worked closely with as students. He was doubtful about it, as were his mother and mine. Everyone warned us that trade unionists neglected their children and had affairs with other women. Unionists also earned very little, so I would have to subsidise his involvement by providing most of the income for our children and home.

His mother Sanna shared these concerns with me, but I laughed and told her that we were different. We were revolutionaries, socialists, who would live by our principles. I was more concerned about where my young lover had disappeared in the man who came home from the New Republic Bank every day talking about money, money, money. In Mala Singh's philosophy class at UDW, my friend Junie and I had been the only two students who gave unconventional answers to the question of what we wanted to achieve after university. Everyone else spoke of respectable marriage, luxury cars and homes, overseas travel, a big bank balance. Junie told me decades later that she had kept a piece of wood I had painted red and carved with the words 'Normality is happiness never reaching ecstasy'. In my marriage, I wanted my Comrade Jayendra back. He began work in the union, and I forgot Sanna's wise warning.

I was teaching in Chatsworth, a township far from Reservoir Hills, where we were staying. It was difficult to co-ordinate travelling to work with the demands of a baby. Jayendra and I had moved to a new flat and we decided to buy a second-hand car. Most of my savings were spent on buying it. The car got stuck shortly

after we drove it into our flat's parking area and it never moved again. A mechanic explained that some parts of the engine had been held together by putty. Without a car, I had to take the bus after teaching and plod up and down a steep hill to a child-minder's home before climbing the four flights of stairs carrying Parusha, her pram and my schoolbag of books. It was not for nothing that Reservoir Hills was part of what was known as the Valley of a Thousand Hills. By then I was pregnant with my second child and I began to hate the stairs. I also suspected that Jayendra was having an affair, but he insisted that I was 'imagining things'. Those years were painful as I wavered between trusting my own intuition and a fear of what 'imagining things' implied about my sanity. Years later, he would confess to the many affairs that had begun that year.

My second baby had a distinctly different personality from Parusha even in my womb. After a few months he was either kicking a ball around or conducting an entire orchestra in there. I laughed when his little foot or hand punched the skin of my stomach. For this birth I knew what to expect and was determined to see him entering the world. Even with my legs trussed up, I leant forward, delighted to see him arrive. The GP was amused. 'This is the first time I saw anyone so determined to see their baby emerge. It must be all the yoga you do.' That night I fought the nurses for the right to have him with me. Then I was too scared to sleep in case I rolled on top of him. I spent my time holding his tiny hands and gazing at his little face. I was out of the hospital the next morning. My mother was waiting with the lamp, the fruit and the brass container of water. Like our daughter, our son also received the blessings of the elements in all four directions as soon as we arrived home. We planted a fruit tree for him, too. There were few names in the book of Hindu names beginning with the letter y that the guru had identified with his time of birth. The one whose sound and meaning resonated most was Yashodan, 'one who helps others'.

In our flat, while I cleaned our bedroom I would put Yashodan (whom I began calling Shod) on the floor of the lounge. He would move his entire little body in greeting the rays of the sun and seemed to talk animatedly to it. In his cot the wooden mobile with its bright yellow, red, blue and green metal bells made him gurgle with pleasure, just as the mobile of butterflies had fascinated Parusha. Parusha wanted to help her little brother do everything and she enthusiastically learnt how to fold his nappies. She also helped Shod when he was crawling to take his first steps. There is a picture of them in the Botanical Gardens, where Parusha loved to feed the ducks; she is trying to help him stand up, both of them concentrating on their huge task.

As a young mother, I could not sustain my activism as before and came to be harshly judgemental of myself. It felt as if I had not slept for ages and I began to think my brain would never work again. I could not complete reading anything without being disturbed – even the toilet was no longer a private space. Reading used to be my refuge and sanctuary. In a study group discussion in our flat, I sat feeling guilty. Everyone else had read a thick wad of photocopied pages on some important theme. In mid-discussion my baby needed to be breastfed and I left, zonked by fatigue. As I write this, I realise that everyone else in the group was male.

In my children's first years, I insisted that Jayendra had, at the very least, to wash the cloth nappies (disposable nappies were simply unaffordable). But he was often away for long periods and I rapidly lost the battle to share parenting and housework with my husband. When I was exhausted and alone with my two little babies, one of whom developed severe colic and could not stop crying, I felt overwhelmed and began to resent Jayendra. I resented the freedom that union work and travelling gave him from most of the everyday chores that I was responsible for, before and after a full day's teaching. I resented his ability to sleep through their cries when he was home. By contrast, I seemed to wake at the

first whimper, my body fine-tuned to my babies' needs beyond my conscious desire for sleep. Parenting became a source of serious tension between my husband and me.

As a young mother trying to balance work, family and political activism, I was drawn to women's organisations in the hope that they would be sensitive to the difficulties I'd met myself. Unfortunately few of them were. Still, some women's meetings were held in our own homes. Shamim Marie recalls one in my flat in 1982, to found *Speak*, the first feminist magazine in South Africa. While we worked, my daughter Parusha, who was just over a year old then, played with Shamim's children and with Sheila Jolobe's son. At the time I was pregnant with Yashodan. In those early days many women's meetings would be held with children playing around us. While trying to change the political, we tried to integrate the personal; for most of us there was little choice.

Six

TEACHING

Outside home, I was fully engaged as a teacher, working at a number of schools as the Department of Indian Affairs transferred me from one school to another. I had strong opinions and ideas. My first year of teaching was the year I turned 21. I firmly opposed replacing one form of propaganda with another, didn't believe that a child was an empty vessel passively waiting to be filled and refused to teach children to memorise and repeat in rote fashion. Opposing corporal punishment, I believed that affirming positive qualities yielded far better results than insults and beatings. My best teachers had nurtured the creative potential in me. As a teacher I wanted to do the same for those I was responsible for by helping develop critical, creative thinking and a love for the poetry and power of words.

In my first year I taught in two schools, including Chatsworth High, where my time was fraught with differences I had with management. One of my English classes, Standard 6E, was also my form class. The ranking of classes from A downwards was theoretically made not on the basis of any assumed inferiority or

superiority. But in practice poorer students were in the majority in the lower-ranking classes and middle-class students dominated the higher ones. On my first day in 6E, the drab classroom reinforced the sense of depression and low self-esteem expressed in the faces and body language of the children. They spent a large portion of their days in this room yet it reflected nothing about them. Surely it was possible to create an environment in which children could learn how to think for themselves and be creative. As I opened up a conversation about the classroom, I looked directly at each child. 'What would make your classroom a place you felt comfortable and happy in?' Tentatively and then excitedly, they started to share their ideas. Finally I asked them to bring something the next day, however small, 'that is special to you'.

The next morning I walked into a transformed classroom. There were small pot plants, shells on some desks, even a little fishbowl on my table. The boy who had brought the fishbowl seemed extremely shy. I welcomed the changes, specifically mentioning the fishbowl, and watched his face light up. After tea, I came back to teach them an English lesson and found a tangible sense of despondency and depression. What had happened? The accountancy teacher had walked in, insulted them and scorned the things they had brought. 'And you, my boy, you will spend the rest of your life swimming round and round aimlessly like your silly goldfish!'

I left the class and went in search of this teacher. He was a tall, genial man who had been pleasant towards me in the staffroom, where I spent most of my free time trying to finish my work so as to clear my afternoons and evenings for Parusha. By the time I'd reached the staffroom, I wanted to strangle him. 'How can you do that to kids who already have all the odds stacked against them?' I demanded when I saw him. He was surprised that anyone would defend them. 'You're new here, so let me give you some advice. Those kids won't listen unless you're hard with them. They have

to be disciplined for their own good.' That's when I lost my temper. 'You bastard! How dare you destroy them and then justify it.'

He was shocked. It was the swear word that did it. Good Indian women teachers never swore. They slapped, pinched and caned, they maliciously insulted little children, but they never ever used bad language, especially not in the sacred space of the staffroom. That night I fantasised about the revolution. This teacher, and all the other mind-numbingly cruel teachers I had met, were lined up against a wall and shot. In dreamtime I was neither peaceful yogi nor Gandhian passive resister.

In this school, as in most others, only the A-class students took part in the annual school play. My school friend Shireen Sabat was also a teacher at the school. Together we approached the English head of department and secured his permission to get the other students involved in short sketches and poetry so that they too would gain the confidence that came from performing on stage.

Eager to audition, children packed the classroom to overflowing. They waited excitedly at the windows and open door. We decided to find ways to accommodate as many as possible and came in to work with them at weekends. Their parents, mainly from the poorer area around the school, made costumes from scrap material. The principal and the head of English finally came to view a rehearsal. The generally sour expression of the principal tightened even more and he left without saying a word. The next day he informed us that the time allocated for the actual performance was no longer available. He avoided looking directly at Shireen or me as he lied to us. Of all the short skits and poetry the children had prepared so painstakingly, only a single poem read by one student was allowed. A member of the management board told me later that in their meeting the principal had described the pieces as too political and instructed them to be blocked. The fairly harmless pieces we had selected were along the lines of Pete Seeger's song 'What did you learn in school today, dear little child of mine?' adapted to South

African conditions. There was nothing particularly revolutionary about any of them.

The 8A class, to whom I also taught English, heard about the principal's ruling and refused to act in the main play. He summoned them and said that Shireen and I would be reported to the Department of Indian Affairs if they did not perform. They had to agree to go ahead with the main play. Shireen and I were summoned separately and told that, if we did not persuade the students to proceed, the principal would send a list of the students to the department for disciplinary action. The main play finally went ahead, with the poem read by the student in front of a closed curtain, during the interval of the main play.

I was still at Chatsworth High when students organised another boycott. I was held responsible by the principal for the students' stand and was transferred to Sastri College. Sastri College, the first school for 'Indian' boys in Natal, which both my father and Daya attended, had initially had been a distinguished institution, but apartheid had designated it a 'catering school', training young boys as waiters, one of the few occupations traditionally open to working-class Indians under apartheid. It was also used as a recruiting ground for the army and the navy, representatives of which were regularly invited to the school. In the staffroom, the only white teacher would boast that the ornament hanging on a chain around his neck was the tooth of a 'terrorist' from his time on the border as a conscripted soldier.

Among my English classes were the Standard 9C boys whom the teachers and the principal disparaged. 'Don't waste your time. Those thugs are the dregs of society, a bunch of useless gangsters, just biding time.' The first day I walked into Standard 9C the boys looked me up and down, in keeping with the stereotype. Many of them were taller than me and some were older. As time went on, I would often take this class to the Botanical Gardens near the college. I would ask these 'thugs and gangsters' to lie on their

backs on the grass and look up at the sky. They slowly relaxed their bodies into the earth as they travelled inside themselves. Then they would sit up and take in the colours and shapes around them and above them. One of the more timid boys, Dhanasagren, finally allowed himself to flow onto the page in his poetry and essays. Later, the inspector who came to observe me teaching in 9C praised the students as 'highly intelligent', producing 'brilliant, creative work'. The principal whispered to me, 'Were you really in the 9C class?' He had asked me to shift classes when the inspector arrived and couldn't believe this man was talking about the same boys that he himself had written off so completely. In this same year Dhanasagren went from shy diffidence to winning the school prize as the top English student out of all the Standard 9 classes in the school.

In an attempt to co-opt Indian and Coloured people into the apartheid system, two extra houses of parliament were set up and elections for the tricameral parliament were held in 1984. I was one of the thousands of activists across South Africa who worked in the anti-tricameral campaign. In many areas we informed pensioners that despite the threats by various candidates, they would not lose their pensions or their homes if they did not vote. 'They have really been frightening us with their stories, you know. But I will not vote,' said a determined, grey-haired woman in a sari. Like her, millions across South Africa buried the tricameral system. On the day of the tricameral elections, 90 per cent of the students in Sastri College staged a stay-away. The next day I was held responsible for the student stay-away and was transferred with immediate effect to Effingham Secondary. I went from class to class to say goodbye on the Friday – I had to report to my new school on the Monday.

In 9C, one of the boys who had initially been most difficult stood up: 'They made a mistake sending you here, didn't they? They never give us good teachers. We knew you wouldn't stay with

us.' There was anger, bitterness and dejection in his voice. I looked around the class at their eyes, at the boys I had found inside the 'gangsters', and realised they all believed that they didn't deserve a good teacher. My appointment must have been a mistake and I must have asked for the transfer. I explained that I hadn't applied for the transfer and had been happy teaching them. I wished I didn't have to leave but had no choice in the matter. They listened quietly, subdued as I said goodbye and wished them well.

Each time I was transferred, I refused to cry, not wanting the principal to know that the department's punitive action had hurt. Now as I walked out of the room, my old resolution shattered. The following week, when I returned to collect some of my books, I overheard the woman teacher who had replaced me. She was teaching Alan Paton's *Cry, the Beloved Country*. 'OK, you can be Khumalo, you're as black as anything,' she said, ridiculing the darkest boy in the class.

At Effingham Secondary, I put out my hand to greet the principal. He looked contemptuously at it without extending his hand. 'I have read your file. Let me tell you one thing straight away, Ms Govender,' he sneered. 'You will not get up to any of your tricks in *my* school.' The principal was a short man, with no light in his eyes. The Standard 5 class that I was assigned to had over 40 children. It was intended as a demotion after teaching Standard 9 and matric. After the first day the naughtiest boy in the class came up to me and pointed out the cane that sat on top of the cupboard. 'Mam, all the other teachers hit us with that cane. You must use it, too.' He was tiny and I wondered at how quickly he had been conditioned. 'No, I don't believe in hitting children.' 'But it's OK, mam, everyone hits us.' 'I know, but I'm not going to.' The class sat up, puzzled at this new approach. By the end of that week we were having fun together.

But the principal was not and he used every petty trick he could think of to make my teaching life difficult. I did not

want to waste my time and energy in this fruitless manner, and resigned. I wrote an honours exam in English and taught at the University of Durban-Westville, while I began a master's thesis focused on 'alternative written media', specifically the garment union's newspaper, *Clothesline*. At the university I also worked as research assistant to the director of the Institute of Social and Economic Research, from whom I learnt valuable research skills. In a Special Branch raid on my parents' home, my thesis materials were confiscated, but this was not the reason I abandoned it. Life as an activist with two young children was demanding and my own inclination was to join the union movement itself, not just study it from afar. But I did not abandon my love of teaching. In the next few years I moved my craft beyond the classroom, onto the factory floor itself.

PART 2

Politics

Seven

SOLIDARITY

I am not sure when I first learnt the slogan 'sisterhood and solidarity'. My first encounter with a progressive women's organisation was in high school when I attended a meeting of the Black Women's Federation, which had been formed by leaders like Winnie Mandela and Fatima Meer. At the meeting, I heard politically articulate women speak of unity between women from all oppressed groups. As a university student, my commitment to the emancipation of women grew as I became involved in community activism in townships like Phoenix. Here women began organising through the Phoenix Women's Circle. I attended several of their meetings and learnt from the women of Phoenix as they campaigned for a crèche and other essentials that few men seemed to care about.

I read about feminists from countries like Zimbabwe, Nicaragua, Cuba and the United States, and learnt of the way powerful men abused power in struggles from civil rights to socialism. I discovered different types of feminisms and identified with feminist socialists, who believed that changing women's lives also entailed changing

political and economic conditions. Most working women balance their responsibilities for caring for their children, cooking and cleaning while they work long, hard hours for poor wages at workplaces where they often experience sexual harassment and lose their jobs for being pregnant. I drew inspiration from Paulo Freire, who in his *Pedagogy of the Oppressed* observed: 'Liberation is like childbirth, and a painful one. The person who emerges is a new person, no longer oppressor or oppressed, but a person in the process of achieving freedom.'

I read Alexandra Kollantai's book *Love of Worker Bees*, which told the personal stories of women asserting their freedom in early Soviet Russia. Kollantai became Commissar for Social Welfare in Lenin's government and used her power to advance the interests of the poorest women, ensuring that the Soviet government committed itself to clinics, nurseries and maternity homes, female suffrage, legal equality, free divorce, free abortion, two months' paid maternity leave, workplace and community crèches, and a law against wife-beating. However, these victories were overturned when Stalin came to power and introduced anti-abortion and anti-divorce laws, outlawed homosexuality, and introduced the Order of Maternal Glory for mothers who had seven or more children. Capitalism completed Stalin's job. Recent United Nations reports reveal that women's lives in the former Soviet Union and Eastern Europe have deteriorated hugely. While writing this book, a feminist from Poland challenged me for using the word 'comrade' affectionately of beloved activist friends. 'In my country, many of the socialists and communists are the bloated party bureaucrats who exploit their positions to build their own power. They are the elite.'

At UDW, my involvement in women's issues deepened when a few of us organised an SRC women's subcommittee, which signed up large numbers of women for self-defence classes against rape and sexual harassment. Some SRC men and women thought that

organising women was divisive to the struggle against apartheid and opposed the committee's formation. While we were organising on our campus, women in the Alan Taylor Residence at the Medical School complained to us that some student leaders had barred their girlfriends from attending political meetings. They demanded that 'their' women, despite the fact that they were also studying to be doctors, should cook and clean for them. Subordination was deeply entrenched and not easily dismantled.

In 1982 the twenty-sixth anniversary of Women's Day was held at St Faith's Cathedral in the centre of Durban. I was among those who gathered to celebrate the march by 20 000 insubordinate African, Indian, Coloured and white women to the Union Buildings in Pretoria to protest against the extension of pass laws to African women. The women had mocked the prime minister, J.G. Strijdom, with the words: *Wathint' abafazi, wathint' imbokodo uzokufa* – 'You have touched the women, you have struck a rock.'

At the celebration at St Faith's I learnt of the recent message of the ANC president, Oliver Tambo, to an ANC women's conference in exile: 'The struggle to conquer oppression in our country is the weaker for the traditionalist, conservative and primitive restraints imposed on women by man-dominated structures within our movement, as also because of equally traditionalist attitudes of surrender and submission on the part of women.' His words struck home, as I was fighting my own battles in my marriage against 'surrender and submission'.

After university I became involved in various local organisations that were trying to organise against patriarchy in different ways. One of these, the Natal Organisation of Women (NOW), founded in 1983, had begun mobilising women in townships in Durban and Pietermaritzburg on issues ranging from civic matters to apartheid violence. The United Democratic Front (UDF), the massive anti-apartheid movement, had just been launched

and NOW became affiliated to it. In the discourse current in opposition politics of that time women were seen as 'a sector', like the youth or workers. Often this approach blurred the fact that while it was strategic to organise women to unite against their own oppression, it was equally important to challenge the sexist practices women experienced as members of political, youth or workers' organisations, which, too often, became characterised as male organisations. Many of us believed that women had to be organised against limitations imposed by the state as well as those prescribed by their own comrades in their organisations and homes. Few male leaders, on the other hand, recognised patriarchy as an enemy within our own ranks.

After my day's work as a teacher and while parenting Parusha and Yashodan, I served NOW on a voluntary basis, co-ordinating media such as pamphlets, newsletters, booklets, posters and even T-shirts. NOW provided an outlet for my love for writing even though it was often done anonymously, in the tradition of the day. As a young mother, I appreciated being able to do much of the media work from our homes, often in Phozo Zondo's home in Lamontville or mine in Clare Estate. One night two of us on the media committee – Pingla Udit and I – went to the UDW hostels to put up posters for a Women's Day meeting. When we'd finished, we found ourselves trapped in the men's hostel. We were lost in the corridors, the gate was locked, and we didn't know the way out. We spent a long time giggling like maniacs as we tried to escape without being spotted by the warden. But there was real danger more often than fun in working against apartheid. When Pingla was detained by the police, she was tortured to the point where she had to be taken to hospital by her interrogators.

I learnt much from the women I worked with and experienced sisterhood and solidarity, not just with those who were my age but with older women such as Victoria Mxenge and Florence Mkhize.

Amid the hard work there was plenty of camaraderie and good humour. At the end of a long trip to Johannesburg, one late hot summer's night, I finally reached Florence's home. As she got out of the car she said, 'Comrade Pregs, you drove so well – just like a man.' An instinctive irritation at the comparison quickly dissolved in Ma Flo's laughter.

Phozo Zondo was NOW's full-time organiser. Tall, with brown, laughing eyes, we became close friends, in a connection that seemed to outlast distance and time. Our work together in the media unit took us to all the different branches across Durban's townships and we had fun together, even during dangerous moments. Once security police brandishing huge guns forced us all onto the floor outside the NOW office. Phozo was hustled into one of NOW's two offices, where she was asked if she was NOW's chairperson. (The chair, Nozizwe Madlala, would later be detained but she was then safe in hiding.) Phozo truthfully denied that she was Nozi. The police took me into the other office and asked if I was Pregs, whom they wanted to question. I insisted I was not. 'Pregs is a boy's name.' I frowned at their ignorance like a stern schoolteacher, knowing the fear this instils in bullies. 'My name is Jewel,' I said in all truth, recalling my childhood nickname. Later, Phozo and I laughed at the policemen's confusion and at the white policewoman with angry eyes, who threatened to hit me.

In July 1985 Victoria Mxenge, our treasurer, was assassinated by apartheid agents outside her home as she unpacked groceries from her car. When I first heard of Victoria's death, I thought this simply could not be true. The image of Victoria laughing a few days earlier kept flitting through my mind. We had just finished NOW's working committee meeting in her office and were in the street downstairs. Victoria, a round, sturdy woman with large spectacles that covered most of her face, had a belly laugh that wrinkled up her eyes – a wonderfully loud, open laugh. None of us realised that we were laughing a slow goodbye.

Before Victoria's assassination, her husband Griffiths had also been kidnapped and hacked to death in 1981 by members of apartheid's death squad. In the month Victoria was murdered the Nationalist government declared a state of emergency, in which they killed 500 people including leaders like Matthew Goniwe, banned political meetings and arrested 14 000 people in three months.

Despite all these efforts, the state did not crush the spirit that had unfolded. Women continued to organise. Regional affiliates of the UDF like NOW talked of uniting nationally through the Federation of South African Women (Fedsaw). Through some of the Fedsaw steering committee meetings which I attended, I met and developed deep respect for a diverse range of feminists from across South Africa, from Feroza Adams in her snazzy short skirt and red lipstick to Sister Bernard Ncube in her austere Catholic habit. We all shared a passionate commitment to changing women's lives. Women had been working hard at all levels of the struggle against apartheid and in many instances in the struggle against patriarchy, too, and had achieved a great deal throughout the country.

The steering committee meetings finally culminated in a date for the relaunch of Fedsaw, which had been dormant since leaders like Lilian Ngoyi were persecuted by the state in the late 1950s. A group of us travelled from Durban to Johannesburg for the great day. There, however, it became clear that a decision had been taken by someone, somewhere, to prevent Fedsaw's re-emergence. Even today, historians documenting this period are unclear about what the motives were. At the time the decision not to re-form Fedsaw was met with confusion, sorrow and anger. When the older women, who had been part of Fedsaw in the 1950s, were told, they wailed out loud. NOW's Thoko Msane, who was to become minister of land affairs in South Africa's democracy, broke into song, a hymn for all of us, that slowly eased the despair.

A short while after the aborted Fedsaw launch, another was planned, this time in Cape Town. NOW hired a taxi kombi and, old and young, we piled into it for the long drive from Durban. When we eventually reached Cape Town, confusion about the launch began all over again. In our long discussions through the night we eventually settled on a compromise. Instead of Fedsaw, the United Democratic Front Women's Congress, Udfwco (pronounced 'Oodufco'), was formed, but it did not last very long. The veteran leader Helen Joseph, who had been invited to deliver the keynote address to relaunch Fedsaw, was informed shortly before she spoke of the change. She looked fragile as she fumbled through the speech.

It remains unclear why both launches were blocked like this. Maybe some powerful men were threatened by the idea of a strong, independent women's organisation. Maybe others were afraid that Winnie Mandela might use the opportunity to entrench personal power through leadership of Fedsaw. At that time Winnie had become embroiled in the kidnapping of Stompie Seipei, a 14-year-old, through her notorious football club. Stompie was subsequently killed.

After the meeting, we climbed back into the taxi, disillusioned and confused. Our journey home did not improve our morale. We had a puncture. The driver got lost in the middle of nowhere late at night. Then, as he continued going round in circles in the dark, he insisted on scaring some of the women with his tales of tokoloshes (mythical evil creatures), and nothing would stop him. Fortunately, neither tokoloshes nor unexplained directives could dampen our spirits for long.

Eight

THE COMMISSAR

In 1987 the Natal Organisation of Women asked me to represent local women at an international women's conference in the Soviet Union. Communism was apartheid's number one enemy; the Soviet Union was condemned as evil incarnate. Despite the obvious dangers, I took the request seriously and felt honoured by the trust of my NOW comrades. We investigated how I could travel to the Soviet Union and back without the authorities knowing: visits to the Soviet Union were then not allowed. We also had a series of meetings, including one with a lawyer, to look at the logistics. It was decided that the safest route would be via London, where the ANC would ensure that I reached the Soviet Union without alerting the apartheid state. I was 27 years old and it was the first time I would be travelling beyond South Africa's borders.

Just before I left, NOW's diligent secretary told me that a comrade, who had been a student with me at UDW and who was now in hiding from the police for ANC underground activities, wanted to meet with me. I respected the comrade, whom I will

call Ahmed (not his real name); he had a good sense of humour and had been one of many young people detained by apartheid's security police in the early 1980s. I parked my car in the parking lot behind the Asherville swimming pool, the secret venue he had chosen, and watched him walk towards me, in his now trademark dark sunglasses. I could not help thinking that he had developed the powerful surreptitious air of a character from a James Bond thriller. After our conversation, Ahmed asked me to buy some bottles of whisky to take to Aziz Pahad, a senior ANC comrade, in London as part of my introduction to him. I was sure Aziz was a nice fellow, but I refused to take him whisky. In a movement where women started as mere bearers of tea and biscuits, it was easy to be pigeonholed. If I met this comrade I wanted it to be on equal terms, not as a bearer of whisky. (As it turned out, I did not get to meet Aziz on this trip.)

Soon after I landed in London, the BBC news showed the opening of the women's conference in the Soviet Union. I was shocked. After all the secrecy about leaving South Africa, someone in the underground had got the dates wrong. The BBC camera didn't just stay with the faces of those on the podium; it panned across the whole room. With that kind of exposure, clearly I could not travel on to the Soviet Union – it would be a one-way ticket to jail back in South Africa. My children Parusha and Yashodan were only five and four years old, and I was not going to take a risk that would separate me from them.

Instead I spent my time at several other meetings in London. I addressed the Anti-Apartheid Movement, and felt I was back in my high-school debating team forcing myself to overcome an inhibiting shyness. I attended the International Conference on Women and Shelter and was impressed by the clarity and passion of the feminist delegates from India. I was intrigued by how insubordinate they were in comparison to the stereotypical oppressed Indian woman. One of them gave me a poster of a woman painted a deep berry shade. She strode forward on the

poster, almost flying in her sari, her hair streaming behind her. The words below read: 'Within the silence of my soul were struck the chords of a new harmony.'

Outside King's Cross station I met the senior communist leader and Jayendra's uncle, M.D. Naidoo, for the first time. He had said on the phone that he would be wearing a black beret. He looked very much the revolutionary intellectual on a secret mission – he knew that the apartheid state had eyes and ears everywhere and many ANC members had lost their lives. His son Sadhan, an agriculturist who ran the ANC's farm in Lusaka, was assassinated by an apartheid agent. His ex-wife Phyllis, a lawyer, helped those who had been subjected to horrific bomb attacks in exile. M.D. had spent many years on Robben Island for his belief in communism and his work against apartheid.

We began talking on the train to his sister's home. I admired the depth of his knowledge and his rigorous analysis. Unfortunately, before long we were in serious disagreement. I had heard that he did not take clashes lightly. Holding my ground won his respect, though, and by the time we arrived there was a warm rapport between us. Photos of us show a smiling, short-haired young woman in a white Indian cotton dress, African wooden beads circling her neck and black tai-chi shoes, sitting alongside a middle-aged bald man with intelligent eyes laughing over his black-rimmed glasses.

Vella Pillay invited me to supper at his house. He was an ANC and SACP member and a respected economist who worked for the Bank of (Communist) China. Vella helped design the ANC's economic policies, which were to be rejected by the ANC in government in favour of ones that deepened rather than eradicated poverty in the new South Africa. Vella's wife Patsy was British, and passionate about South Africa. Her kindness and ease quickly made me feel at home.

The meeting that led to all the trouble for me later on was a breakfast session with Wally Serote and Reg September. There

was a great deal of secrecy about the venue, a coffee shop in a remote part of London. I asked Kumi Naidoo, my trusted friend and comrade who'd fled from the South African Police earlier that year, to accompany me. Over tea and sandwiches, Wally calmly said, 'We want you to set up the ANC MK unit in Swaziland.' The underground unit they were asking me to re-establish had recently been smashed by the South African Defence Force. I thought I must have misheard. I'd taught at schools and university, worked as a researcher, and had absolutely no training for what they were asking me to do. I said I was an above-ground operative, and best at working at this level with trade union and women's movements. Afterwards, Kumi and I laughed and agreed that the idea of my re-establishing the Swaziland unit was completely crazy. Years later, in parliament, Wally told me that after our meeting he'd tried to arrange for me to leave South Africa for military training, and one of those he had sent messages with was Kumi. When I asked Kumi why he hadn't passed on Wally's messages, he explained that he knew I wouldn't, under any circumstances, leave my children.

After our breakfast meeting Wally and Reg drove us through a typically wet, grey London day. As we slowed down at a traffic light, a car banged into us and a briefcase at the back of our car hit me hard on my head. I was concussed for a while but was touched by the genuine concern of both these older men, who drove me to a public hospital despite their earlier concern about secrecy.

On my return from London, Jayendra met me at the airport in Johannesburg and confessed to the affairs he had had since my second pregnancy five years earlier, which he had previously denied. It was painful hearing that all the women he named were comrades I knew, including a close friend. Still, it was a relief to know I had not imagined Jayendra's affairs, as he had always claimed. Soon afterwards I asked him to move out of our flat, and lived alone

with our children. After they were asleep, I would write and write, pouring my heart out onto the page. The separation was not a clean break – our emotional entanglement with each other would take a while longer to unravel. The year 1987 marked the time when I reclaimed my self, stopped being a naive, gullible victim in my marriage and left all marital convention behind. That year I fell in love with another man (who remains a good friend).

It was dark when my connecting flight from Johannesburg landed in Durban. I had missed my children terribly and just wanted to hold them close. They were fast asleep when I crept into their bed and lay between them, the warmth of their little bodies quietly comforting. Later, while Jayendra's mother Sanna and I shared a pot of tea in the kitchen, there was a knock at the door. It was Ahmed, who had come to see me. Sanna left the two of us together. He immediately asked for a report of the people I had met in London and what the meetings were about. It was late – past midnight. I was feeling physically ill, exhausted and emotionally drained. 'You can't be serious,' I laughed, my usual reflex in difficult moments.

He was furious. 'How dare you laugh? Do you know who I am and what I can do?'

'Of course I know who you are. You're Ahmed.' I was tired and disliked the bullying tone in his voice. Ahmed had changed since university in ways that were not pleasant. I refused to give him a report. 'Why do you need to know?' The next day he arrived with a fax which he claimed had come directly from the ANC in Lusaka. He waved it in the air, excitedly exclaiming that he did not need me to tell him whom I had met; he would find out everything anyway. Without allowing me to read the fax for myself, he proceeded to read it to me. It said that Reg and Wally had broken ANC procedure by not going through the command structures inside the country. This would be used as a test case to ensure that Wally and Reg's 'disobedience' would never be repeated by them

or anyone else again. Was I to be a guinea pig in a test case?

I couldn't believe what I was hearing – that this was how the ANC underground would operate. I had been clear that I was not going to proceed with the request from Wally and Reg about re-establishing the Swaziland unit but was nonetheless shocked that the ANC would use this experience as a test case without clarifying what my response had been. I did not believe that the ANC could entrust such power to Ahmed, who was not yet 30, and had a tendency to boastfulness that was at odds with work that needed to be kept secret. Despite my instinctive questioning, Ahmed insisted that he was now my commissar and I was answerable to him. In that instant I became part of a two-person underground unit with Ahmed as the one whose orders I was expected to follow and to whom I was answerable. My refusal to submit meekly to his authority, as I was expected to do, would have dire consequences. If I had been less exhausted by everything else that was happening in my life, perhaps I would have challenged him and insisted on a copy of his fax, to study it for myself.

Ahmed's self-assumed role led to unwanted late-night visits to my home. On one such visit, he brought a large paper shopping bag filled with money which he ostentatiously riffled through, telling me he was about to pay ANC operatives. He told me that 'they' could make me 'the most powerful woman in the country'. A lack of ambition for position was probably my greatest protection against such offers.

He would often arrive in smart hired cars very late at night and shine the headlamps into my bedroom, which faced the parking area. I was generally exhausted, not only from the emotional battle with my husband but also from caring for two very young children. I would lie in bed pretending to be asleep, for what felt like forever, before his lights finally moved away. One morning there was a hand-scrawled note under my windscreen wiper. 'Who the hell do you think you are?'

Nine

AN INJURY TO ONE IS
AN INJURY TO ALL

In 1987 my determination to work with garment women workers finally resulted in success. I had been rejected earlier that same year by the Garment Workers' Industrial Union (GWIU) for being 'too political'. Later that year, I again applied for a position with the same union, this time as media officer, and was called to an interview. As the interview drew to a close, I heard one of the old women leaders, Bubbles, whisper loudly to the others, 'She's definitely the best candidate.' I had to keep my delight from showing. Although I was employed as the union's media officer, I was expected to work on everything from education work to organising. I loved all of it. One of my colleagues was Yusuf (not his real name), whom I also knew from our student days at UDW. Like other comrades across South Africa who were already working in the different garment unions, he was trying to transform the GWIU into a progressive body. Initially we built a good working relationship.

At that time GWIU was a 'sweetheart union', cosying up to management rather than protecting workers. There was little

regard for health and safety standards, and few if any maternity rights. Women often hid their pregnancies for fear of losing their jobs. Workers were earning peanuts in most factories: the average wage for skilled workers, the machinists, was R2.21 per hour, and the unskilled earned far less. Management argued that since the clothing workers were mainly women, what they took home after a gruelling week was 'pocket money'. Setting aside the principle of fair pay, the truth was that the women supported not only children and parents but also unemployed husbands – then, as now, unemployment was widespread. Their wages covered rent, food, school uniforms and books, transport, and health care. I felt passionate about changing such conditions.

After two women were strip-searched at one of Durban's largest clothing factories, I initiated GWIU's first campaign against this practice. Even progressive men in the union had not tackled this issue, perhaps because the impact on women's lives was their blind spot. I met shop stewards at the factory and we planned a lunchtime meeting in the canteen where workers could share their experiences and discuss the action they wanted to take. At the meeting, one woman after another got onto the table, our makeshift platform. Strip-searching had been routine practice in the industry for years, and this was their first opportunity to address it. Old and young women talked about their humiliation. One of the oldest women in the factory said hesitantly that she had never told anyone before how awful this experience was for her. 'It was horrible – a stranger's hands inside you.' Many of the women cried when they talked but there was an air of determination that this was the last time they would be humiliated.

The meeting was a catalyst for resistance as the women wanted action. Among other demands they insisted on a written apology from management and a letter declaring the innocence of the two women accused of theft on the factory's public noticeboard. A statement to say 'Sorry, we made a mistake' was the most heartfelt

demand – such a simple thing, such a huge thing, the recognition of their dignity and the integrity of their bodies.

Over the next few weeks, meetings with the women shop stewards helped ensure that they were well prepared, with notes of cases they had investigated. We then met with the personnel manager. He was used to dealing with compliant union officials and was taken aback when I insisted that shop stewards be present. Some of the women put on extra perfume, eye-shadow and lipstick especially for their first meeting with management. In the first few minutes he persisted in addressing me, and ignored the workers. I proposed that we select a chairperson, which the worker leaders promptly did, while I volunteered to take notes. The manager defended the strip-searching. 'There is a lot of theft – it affects the company's profits. This way the workers know that they cannot hide clothing away. They will be searched.' The shop stewards challenged him, describing how the security guards examined the women, which involved searching inside their vaginas. They argued for the rights of women workers over their bodies.

After a short while the manager, exasperated, ignored the shop stewards and turned to me. 'Ms Govender, we do it decently. We have women security guards, and workers are taken into a separate room.' By then I had registered his disgust, his mouth curled into a sneer, at the tight dress of one shop steward, at another's bright blue eye-shadow, his nostrils flaring at the perfume in his antiseptic office. I was angry and blurted out, 'Would you allow your mother, your daughter or your wife to be subjected to one of your searches?'

His response was quick and angry. 'How dare you bring them into this? How dare you compare them to these ... these workers?' His face was an angry red. He too did not think before he spoke.

At the end of the day on Friday, workers joined hands as they marched out of the factory, singing loudly. No one dared stop and search anyone. I was standing outside the factory and watched

them emerge triumphant, Indian and African women holding hands, singing 'Nkosi Sikelel' iAfrika', the Indian women quickly learning the words from their African comrades at a time when the ANC and its anthem were banned. That night the laundry workers on night shift were severely punished by being locked in without access to toilets or canteens. But management had underestimated the solidarity that had emerged – they were soon taught they could not get away with the old 'divide and rule' tactics. The story of what they had done to the laundry workers spread, but it did not create fear. Instead, it seemed to inspire others in this factory to unite in their refusal to be searched.

Despite management's hostile response, workers pioneered creative new strategies in factories across Durban to put an end to strip-searching. Rita Bantjies, who went on to chair the union's regional shop stewards' council, worked at an underwear factory. When it was time to check out, workers refused to leave the factory floor. Instead, they summoned the manager. When he entered, the women opened their blouses revealing their breasts; some even pulled down their panties exposing their backsides. Rita laughed long and loud as she described this to me. 'Come, come, search us now,' they taunted him. These were their bodies. Only they could open their blouses, pull down their panties: no one else dared touch them. The manager had used guards to conduct the strip-searching. Now, for the first time, he saw for himself exactly what was involved. He turned and fled, to howls of laughter. The workers won in this factory even before any written agreement was negotiated. Management stopped strip-searching the workers.

Meeting in Durban's humidity in December 1987, the clothing unions of the Western and Eastern Cape merged with the union in Natal to form the Garment and Allied Workers' Union (Gawu). The Western Cape workers created a new song that everyone

quickly learnt: *Klim op die wa / Almal wat vir Gawu lief het / Klim op Gawu se wa* (Climb on the wagon / Everyone who loves Gawu / Climb on Gawu's wagon). A powerful team of national and regional leaders was put in place. I was elected as national educator and was proud to be part of the team though I felt disconcerted that all the other national and regional officials were men, making me the only woman on the central executive committee. In those days leadership of the trade union movement, as of political movements, was dominated by men. Even when the Congress of South African Trade Unions (Cosatu) was launched in 1985, all the office-bearers were men.

At Gawu's launch, my work was outlined in one of the resolutions: 'An education programme must be developed to ensure that the workers give the union a mandate to join Cosatu.' At that time Cosatu's offices were being bombed, its members detained across the country, the rank and file fired on with live ammunition, the leadership vilified by state media. But many of the union's Coloured workers in the Western Cape referred derogatorily to Cosatu as die *kaffir-unie* (the kaffir union). One of the huge challenges in developing an education programme to fulfil the union's mandate would be the prejudice, fear and division that apartheid had entrenched.

Building unity within the union was not a smooth, easy process. During a lunch meeting about a strike at one of Durban's large factories on the South Coast, a woman worker stood up and shouted: 'You can't trust the Indians. They won't join us. They only say they will join us now, but when the time comes we Africans will be standing alone.' These were insults about Indian workers who had already committed themselves to joining the strike together with African workers. Njengabantu (Nje) Sithole, my organising partner in the union, and I jumped onto the table and talked simultaneously, in Zulu and English. Nje and I were not translating for each other but we discovered later (as we often

did) that we had said the same things. 'No, Indian and African workers have both voted to strike together. The decision to unite is taken. The bosses and this government always divide us – that is their weapon. Our weapon is our unity. Don't speak the language of division.' There were loud cheers and shouts of 'Amandla!' from both Indian and African workers. In another factory, an Indian manager screamed: 'Stop stirring up my workers. What is wrong with you? You are an Indian like me and you are siding with these raw Africans.' He ran at me with a gun and ordered me out of his factory.

Our first objective as the union leadership was to elect shop stewards and build democratic structures from factory level upwards. The education programme would be tested immediately. In developing the education plan I linked creativity, silent reflection, theory and analysis to practical strategies such as Gawu's Living Wage campaign. The workshops were structured around questions that made shop stewards think about how the apartheid state had divided them and why; the ways in which they internalised the messages they read, heard and saw in state-run media; and around power within the self and collective power.

In the national workshop for the union's leadership I introduced a game about three groups of people – those who owned the wealth, the middle group of professionals such as teachers and doctors, and the group of workers in factories and on farms. At the end of the game, both the worker leaders and the officials reacted with shocked laughter as they reflected on their own behaviour. They realised that, once in the capitalist group, even those who saw themselves as strong socialists rushed to accumulate as much as they could. They described their newly uncovered selves as greedy and exploitative. It was much easier to confront the greed of apartheid's capitalists than our own. Yet in democratic South Africa we would have little choice but to begin addressing this uncomfortable issue.

As national educator a major concern of mine was to develop and empower women within the union. On top of poor wages and working conditions, women often had to endure sexual harassment and strip-searching and were still expected to be sweetly submissive. Their reward was to be selected by the bosses as queen for a day, in the industry's much-publicised Spring Queen competition. For many women, a leader was a man whom they could look up to, not someone who looked like themselves. Although women formed the overwhelming majority of workers in the industry, they seldom elected other women into leadership positions, at factory, regional or national levels.

On the night we gathered for the first workshop I organised for women leaders, everyone shared their ideas and images of women. I wrote the responses onto a large chart: 'women are gossips', they 'bitch about each other', they are 'jealous', they 'pull you down', they 'can't unite over anything', 'never trust a woman' – a depressing litany of all the stereotypes we are told we are. I suggested that if this was what we believed of women, it was what we believed of ourselves, because we *were* women.

'Ag, no,' said one of the participants, 'that's not about us – it's about other women.'

'Yes, but if that's what we believe about other women, then we might as well pack up and go home, because this union is overwhelmingly female. And it is women who will have to unite and act to change conditions.'

An intense discussion followed. The women leaders reflected on how they internalised society's beliefs, which prevented their acting together to change their lives and the lives of their daughters. Around the room, women recounted experiences from girlhood onwards that weakened the sense of self – beatings by parents and then husbands, single parenting, the double load of

work at home and factory, the triple load with union work, sexual harassment, rape. Tragically, almost everyone had similar stories of pain, as children and adults.

Instead of using collective power to solve these problems, however, women sometimes became embroiled in power play, often driven by men, which threatened to destroy their unity. The 1988 Cosatu women's conference fought bitterly on whether to have women's committees in Cosatu or a national women's organisation. Unions mobilised in two opposing groups led by the metalworkers' union, Numsa, and the mineworkers' union, NUM, which proposed rival resolutions. They labelled each other 'workerists' and 'populists', swear words designed to create prejudice and division. It was an extremely tense time.

Lucille Meyer (a unionist who became a senior manager in the Presidency after 1994) and I were finally asked by both groups to work on a compromise resolution. There was value in both resolutions and we agreed that we should draft something that would move us out of the conflict so union women could proceed constructively. The final resolution we drafted called for structures within Cosatu to address the problems facing women workers specifically, in the workplace and in the union, as well as a structure to help unite women in the community.

Principled unity, not division, served the best interests of women in our unions and communities. In Gawu, building such unity changed the face of the leadership. Women learnt to support and elect other women into positions of leadership in an unprecedented manner. Within the course of two years, the leadership from factory level to national level became overwhelmingly female, truly representative of the membership.

One of the biggest challenges confronting women in the union was the patriarchy of the state, of their own comrades in the

unions and in the political struggle, and in their own families. I knew from my own experience how difficult it was to address women's oppression, linked as it was to the traditional roles of men and women. Both apartheid's soldiers and the men in our movement shared the belief that their job was to change the world while women's role was to care for children and home. Jayendra and I were both serving as national education officers in our respective unions. Yet, despite my efforts to change the situation, I carried responsibility, like most women, as primary parent and housekeeper, and had to balance this against the demands of my formal paid work.

On a typical day after returning to Durban, having run a workshop for the union elsewhere, I would fetch our children from my parents or Jayendra's mother Sanna. At home I'd find that he had left dishes piled in the sink, beds to be made, and dust and dirt to be swept away. First, though, Parusha and Yashodan had to be bathed – Parusha recalls how she loved the massage that followed – and put to bed. Once there, they needed their favourite songs sung: 'So sleep little one, your day is done, your troubles far behind. Umdokwe, umdokwe, umabhela.' When they finally fell asleep their school uniforms had to be ironed for the next morning. Balancing what sometimes felt like impossible demands, there were nights when their young mother cried herself to sleep.

Of course it was not all tears and fights at home. We often held the most wonderful parties in our flats. But even then the old inequalities popped up at times. At one party, I remember, I'd really enjoyed myself dancing. Afterwards, in the early hours of the morning, I asked those still around to help us clean up. A fellow unionist was furious. He was drunk but I was still unprepared for the way he lashed out: 'You want your husband under your petticoat. You expect a man to sweep, wash napkins and look after babies. I will not do this woman's work. This is not our culture. All

these ideas won't work here.' I teased him gently about his sexism but nothing helped lighten his fury that the old chauvinism was under threat everywhere, even at dancing parties.

Ten

INSUBORDINATION

While I worked in the trade union, Ahmed asked me to write reports on important figures in the movement: the general secretary of Cosatu, Jay Naidoo; the general secretary of Numsa, Alec Erwin; and, amid all the upheaval in my personal life, Jayendra himself. In our interactions, Ahmed fluctuated between charm and rage. I'd laugh at the jokes of this comrade from university days but was stunned by his impatient anger when I kept refusing to write the reports he requested. 'We are fighting the state, not each other. Our priority should be monitoring and reporting their atrocities,' I would argue, aware of how reports on comrades could be used against them. My consistent refusal to write these reports became a major sticking point that seemed to enrage my commissar.

In the union, serious differences also began to emerge between Yusuf and me. It appeared to me as if Ahmed and Yusuf were playing good cop and bad cop in these conflicts. There seemed to be a blurring of lines between underground work and our work in the trade union, as workers were asked to spy on each other with the promise of jobs in the union. Nepotism became evident in the

awarding of lucrative union contracts.

Two women leaders who refused to obey a directive that Yusuf said came from the ANC were attacked in their absence at an organisers' meeting. Attacks like these travelled quickly along the grapevine, and by the time they reached the townships, the label would have become 'impimpi'. This was extremely dangerous and I acted quickly to protect them by asking Harry Gwala, a veteran ANC and Communist Party leader, to intervene to stop the labelling. One of Yusuf's lackeys in Durban complained to the other regional secretaries that I was 'teaching the workers to ask too many questions', a criticism I took as a compliment.

All these differences and more, between Yusuf and me, came to a head in 1988. After working hectically without an administrator for quite some time, the union's executive committee finally decided that an administrator should be appointed to assist me. Interviews were conducted by the national administrator and me and were finalised with Gawu's general secretary. The young woman appointed was a teacher, Prani Raidoo, whose boyfriend had been brutally murdered by apartheid soldiers shortly before. One of the first things Prani did was to help me organise the national leadership workshop. To get a mandate from all the Gawu regions for joining Cosatu, we needed to broaden and intensify our campaign in an integrated fashion.

The leadership workshop was set for the first weekend after the annual holidays. Yusuf was sceptical: 'No one will pitch. Everyone will still be on holiday.' He was still on holiday himself and neglected to attend. I arrived in Cape Town to find everyone present excluding Yusuf. The Cape Town office was organised: led by Lionel October as regional secretary, the region had built the strongest democratic structures through experienced unionists like media officer Ronald Bernickow (Bernie), young energetic organisers like Mario Wanza and Debbie de Vries, and shop stewards like Connie September. The national leadership

workshop, held in the Cape Town office, was a resounding success and I returned to Durban confident that we were on track to secure the mandate.

On the following Monday I was called into Yusuf's office. The success of the national workshop that we'd had in his absence clearly irked him. He was angry but said nothing about the workshop. Instead, he questioned Prani's appointment without his approval, which had not been required. My answer did not placate him. Instead he got angrier as I talked. Ordering me to get rid of Prani, Yusuf grabbed me by the collar of my shirt and swore loudly as he shoved and manhandled me out of his office. Yusuf is not a large man and I am not a small woman but his attack caught me by surprise.

In Jean Lombard's adjoining office I sat down and tried to make sense of what he had just done. I tried to keep myself from crying. This was a trade union; I had been teaching workers, especially women, to stand up for their rights. I decided to take action and wrote a letter calling for disciplinary action against Yusuf for 'verbal and physical assault', which Jean faxed to the general secretary.

Soon afterwards I was informed that there would be a meeting 'with the ANC' to discuss the issue and I was ordered to attend. The meeting was held at Yusuf's house. When I entered Yusuf immediately redirected me to another room where he wanted us to agree on what we were going to report to the meeting. I stood dumbfounded at the door – it was a bedroom. The situation was surreal. This was the man I wanted to charge and he wanted to 'get our story straight' in his bedroom.

In the lounge, seated around his table, were a small group of comrades including Ahmed. The disciplinary meeting addressing a case of 'physical and verbal assault' consisted entirely of Indian men. In the end they concluded that I had provoked Yusuf's behaviour. No one spoke in my defence and I was instructed to drop the call for disciplinary action. I was too exhausted to pursue the call against such strong forces, knowing full well I would not

succeed. All I managed to do was protect Prani, who continued in her job as my administrator for as long as I was national educator. Lionel October, who was in Durban for meetings and had stayed at Yusuf's home, was horrified. 'God, they operate like the bloody Mafia. If I had not seen them in action, I would never have believed the things they get up to.'

Later on, my brother Pat found out what Yusuf had done. When he stood up for me, he met with the blunt response: 'Don't mess with us. Do you know who we are?' Pat would pay for his stand on behalf of his sister by earning the wrath of men with powerful networks across the country, which they were not ashamed to use.

Things went from bad to worse for me in Gawu. The organisers and the administrative staff were warned not to speak to me. Almost all the Indian organisers seemed to obey the directive while the Indian administrative staff in our office continued to greet me unless someone else was there, when they too froze, fearful of those with power over them. Ostracism was a powerful weapon.

As the tension heightened, I got thinner and thinner, even though I still had a ravenous appetite. One day as I stuck into a 'bunny-chow' (half a loaf of bread stuffed with curry), Natal's regional educator, who seemed to take perverse delight in being mean, burst out, 'What's wrong with you, eh? Do you have Aids or what?' (The disease had only just begun to be mentioned in South Africa and already carried great social stigma.) The stress of conflict in the union, in the unit with my commissar, and in my marriage, together with the intensity of our education programme and the work involved in caring for two young children, was taking its toll. I was admitted to hospital, not with the gastric flu the union doctor had diagnosed but with a serious kidney complaint. The doctor told me to take a month's leave to enable my body to

heal properly. Working to the point of illness was a pattern that was not easy to change. I returned to work long before the month was up because of the urgent things that had to be done.

◎

The education programme helped secure a unanimous mandate from Gawu's workers to join the non-racial trade union federation, Cosatu. The first step towards becoming part of Cosatu was to merge with the Cosatu union in our sector, the Amalgamated Clothing and Textile Workers' Union (Actwusa). As we drew closer to the merger, competition between the two unions heightened. At one point Yusuf and the Gawu regional secretary (a massively built man, over six feet tall) were chased out of a factory by knife-wielding Actwusa members. 'Shit, I thought we were going to die today!' Yusuf exclaimed, describing how the workers had shaken their car. At the next organisers' meeting he asked me to leave education work to help the organising department get through this 'crisis', motivating that this had been agreed to by Gawu's general secretary. I accepted the mandate.

With Nje Sithole, I was allocated the factories that were no-go zones for Gawu in Durban, including the one Yusuf had been chased from. I was happy to work in the factories again with Nje. The workers attended our lunchtime meetings with knives clearly visible. Nje and I opened discussions about wages, working conditions and other problems in the factory. We asked questions and listened carefully to the answers. When the workers challenged us, we made no excuses or promises. The knives slowly disappeared. All these factories joined Gawu and some of the most antagonistic workers became Gawu shop stewards.

While Nje and I were hard at work at this task, Yusuf informed our general secretary, in a motivation for my dismissal, that I was neglecting my job as national educator. When the central executive committee met in Durban, I described the mandate I

had been given and the work I had been doing. The committee decided that I should continue working as national educator.

There were consequences for being insubordinate to those who have guns, bands of unquestioning followers and important positions. The regional secretaries of the Western and Eastern Cape were informed that the ANC's High Command had instructed that I be removed from the union. I investigated this order by meeting with the ANC veteran Natoo Babenia. 'It's utter nonsense!' he exclaimed and advised me to see Harry Gwala, who had just been released after many years on Robben Island. Lionel October and I drove through the township of Edenvale to find Gwala, who heartily embraced me with arms that no longer functioned. I sat next to him, overwhelmed by the immense compassion he exuded.

Lionel and I queried the ANC directive and Gwala was absolutely clear in his response: 'That is not how the ANC works. It is a lie that the ANC High Command has issued such a directive.' And his advice? 'You just keep doing what you are doing. Do not let them stop you. You are doing the work of the ANC.' He chuckled at our serious faces.

Gwala became a source of comfort. While Yusuf and Ahmed claimed to have all contact with the ANC 'sewn up', it was a relief to know that someone of Gwala's stature in the movement was prepared to meet us and listen to our side of the story. Lionel took others in the union, like Bernie, who later worked on the National Peace Accord, to meet with Gwala. I invited Gwala to speak to workers at an education workshop. Although Yusuf was unhappy, the workers loved Gwala and his speech was interspersed with wild cheering and spontaneous applause.

Yusuf's coterie was confident that he would be appointed the general secretary of the new union to be formed from the merger of

Gawu and Actwusa; this would be called Sactwu, the South African Clothing and Textile Workers' Union. Shop stewards were issued with a directive that the UDF and ANC wanted Yusuf in that post. We again met with Gwala for his guidance. He was angry that the name of the ANC was being used in this way. 'No one has the right to prostitute the name of the movement. Organisations must choose who they want on the basis of clear criteria and what will build and advance the organisation.' And the organisation had chosen. A 'pre-election' meeting of shop steward delegates from every region was held to vote on whom they wanted to lead the new union – and they unanimously elected Lionel October.

At this time, Gwala asked me to write a note describing the power play around the position of general secretary in Gawu. Later he gave me a copy of a fax from John Nkadimeng, one of the South African Congress of Trade Unions (Sactu) leaders in exile: 'We have received the note sent to us over the oncoming elections for a General Secretary candidate for the coming merger between Gawu and Actwusa with great concern. It is true that the movement does not and will never impose its will or a candidate on the people, more especially in a working-class organisation such as a trade union, where democratic elections must be held and respected.'

Gwala also gave me a copy of a fax from the respected UDF lawyer Dullah Omar, in which he undertook to arrange a meeting between Gawu and UDF leadership on the issue. 'We have had some urgent discussions last night. The parties directly involved here in Cape Town are aware of our position and we are hoping that steps can be taken urgently – over the weekend – to bring some sense into the situation.' The internal UDF leadership, including Trevor Manuel, Valli Moosa and Cyril Ramaphosa, met with several of us, including Lionel October and Yusuf. They reiterated the ANC position articulated by Nkadimeng. As a result Yusuf's side agreed to stop their lobbying for his election.

Nonetheless, hustling for position and power reached a new peak. Aware that our shop stewards had chosen October, Actwusa developed a shrewd strategy. In Sactwu, Yusuf would retain a senior position but Desmond Sampson, Gawu's former general secretary, would be elected as the general secretary of the new union with his more powerful counterpart in Actwusa as his assistant. As Western Cape comrades argued, the plan was to have someone who would be 'putty in the hands of Actwusa's general secretary'. As we had the largest membership of the two unions, Actwusa began to campaign in Gawu's factories for Desmond. This was a clever ploy, as our much larger membership would determine the final outcome and Gawu factories were the decisive factor. For me, what mattered more than the individuals was that those chosen to lead should be both capable and principled. In the education programme I did not deal with any of the individuals but rather with the values which should underpin our choice of leader. This was the view I put across in our pamphlets, workshops, in factories and on the buses to congress.

At the inaugural congress of Sactwu, held in Cape Town, Yusuf's group of supporters were supremely confident, as was the Actwusa leadership, that Desmond Sampson would win the majority vote. Instead, when the election results were announced, Lionel October was elected general secretary by an overwhelming majority. A camera captured Yusuf with his head in his hands and Actwusa's general secretary with his mouth wide open in surprise. The trip back home was not pleasant: Yusuf's coterie saw the defeat as betrayal by the mass of workers who voted and I was treated as a traitor, even though the person who had been democratically elected was an ANC man. Back in Durban, Actwusa's old leader advised me that their 'guys would never forgive me for their defeat'. I was advised to 'go to the gym, go shopping, do anything but run a single education programme or go to a single factory'. Yusuf reiterated the message and for the rest of my time in the

union I could no longer do the work I loved. No matter which side they were on, the patriarchs would not tolerate insubordination, especially not from a woman.

Eleven

BAMBOO

The year 1990 was a turning point for me. It was the year Njengabantu Sithole, my organising comrade, died. The last time I saw Nje was when I was on my way to Cape Town for a weekend workshop. As I said goodbye to him, he pointed at my T-shirt and laughed.

'I want that T-shirt!'

'Too bad,' I laughed back at him. 'You can't have it.'

'But it was made for me.' He read the words *Hasta Victoria la Sempre*, 'Victory is certain'.

'Well, maybe I'll change my mind when I come back on Monday and give it to you,' I teased him as I left. I fetched Parusha and Yashodan, settled them at my parents' home, and caught my plane. My children were laughing when I kissed them goodbye – I left them playing on the tree in the garden with their cousin Karlind, far away in imaginary lands of dinosaurs and dragons.

On Sunday when I returned from Cape Town and fetched my children I learnt that Nje was dead, not from the IFP hit squads who had his name at the top of their hit list of KwaMashu activists,

but from a heart attack. Nje, who had ducked death so many times, had been in and out of detention, tortured and even shot, died at a party while in a swimming pool.

In the office the next morning I was sitting trying to come to terms with Nje's death when Hans, a comrade from Pietermaritzburg, walked past.

'Howzit, Pregs. I'm coming to the meeting to organise the funeral for Nje. Where is it?'

'A meeting? I don't know, Hans. Can I come to it?'

'Of course, you must.'

We walked together down the corridor and turned into the office full of people. The meeting had already started. Yusuf stopped the meeting and looked at me. 'Can you leave, please? This is a closed meeting.' The 'please' was not polite: it was a cold order. The meeting was silent.

'Leave now, please, so we can continue.' His voice broke through my shock. I got up, pushed my chair quietly back and walked out of the door to my office. Behind the screen that blocked my space off from the other offices, I held my pen and started to write, willing myself not to cry as I wrote to Nje, creating a poem to celebrate his life.

A short while later, Nje's girlfriend came to see me. 'I am so sorry that Yusuf ordered you to leave. Nje would have wanted you there. You know Nje loved you so much. You were real comrades. He used to come home every day and talk about what you did together in the factories.' She read my poem quietly. 'You must read this in the church.'

'No, it's for Nje. It belongs to him. You keep it for him.'

She reached into her bag and pulled out a photo of Nje with a friend of his. In the photo, Nje looked relaxed, sitting on the floor, his arm around his friend. 'You can keep the photo. He knew what they were doing to you. He would get so angry at them. Why didn't you talk to him?'

'We were so busy working, there was no time to talk about the shitty things happening and I wouldn't have known where to start. I loved working with Nje – we would laugh so much, I would forget all the crap they were doing.'

'You should have talked to him,' she said, shaking her head.

'Perhaps I should have, but I didn't want to get him into trouble. I knew they didn't appreciate him. They didn't know who he was, his gentle genius. I didn't want him to go against them and experience their viciousness on top of what he'd been through.'

At the funeral I stood outside St Anthony's church. One of the unionists pronounced that the places inside were reserved for family and important guests. I did not go into my old school church to say goodbye to Nje.

Afterwards I joined the African shop stewards and organisers who travelled to his home and his burial. I held my comrades' hands as we sang 'Hamba kahle, Nje, hamba kahle' (Go well, Nje). Phozo and Rita were by my side. Many of those around us were angry that the Indian officials of the union who were prominent at the church funeral were not present at the graveside. 'They did not really love him. They had no respect for him. If they did they would be here, where it matters.' We took turns throwing sand into Nje's grave as we sang 'Hamba kahle, Nje, hamba kahle.'

A few weeks later, on 11 February, Nelson Mandela walked to freedom after 27 years of imprisonment on Robben Island. Activists packed the hall in Diakonia in Durban to watch his release on a large public television screen. The country and the world were captivated by this man of mythic stature, and so was I – but my six-year-old son Yashodan was not enthralled at sitting in a packed hall watching television. Instead, he played outside, running up and down the narrow hallways. A man rushing round the corner collided with him, and his full adult weight lifted

my child into the air. I ran to him but was too late to stop him crashing down onto the cement floor. His head was bleeding, so we rushed him to King Edward Hospital. Fortunately it was not as serious as I'd feared. Once he was treated we went home and I watched Mandela's wonderful first steps much later that night, when my children were fast asleep.

Shortly afterwards I applied for a transfer to the Western Cape. Initially my application was 'mislaid' in the Durban office by the union's regional secretary. Fortunately, I had also handed a copy to Rita Bantjies, who was then chair of the executive committee. She was very supportive. 'If this is what you want, Pregs, the workers will make sure you get the transfer.' She paused. 'I just want to be clear that it is what you want to do, not what they are forcing you to do.' She looked searchingly at me, her big, beautiful eyes quiet and serious. It was my decision to leave Durban, but it was motivated by the reality that if I was to survive, I had to leave my hometown. In the union there was no space to do the work I loved, and at home things had become extremely difficult.

It was not an easy transition. I had to uproot my two young children from their family, friends and school, leave the remnants of my marriage and make a new home in a strange city. My children and I were unhappy at leaving Durban's long summer behind. Autumn and winter in Durban were warm by comparison to Cape Town's howling southeaster and freezing winters.

When we arrived in Cape Town it was frustrating trying to find a new home. White estate agents safeguarded areas against those who were not white. In so-called Coloured and Indian areas, I encountered the same prejudice because we were not Muslim. Initially we lived with my brother Pat, who had married his childhood sweetheart Radha and had a young son, Kamil, whose name means 'complete in all respects'. They welcomed us warmly into their home while I searched for a place of our own. Like me, Pat and Radha were raising their child outside any religious

institution, without belief in God, yet with a profound belief in and practice of the power of love. When their second child arrived they called her Nirvana, meaning 'bliss', an apt name for the love we experienced in their household.

Settling into Cape Town, there were often times when I felt overwhelmed and insecure about my parenting, despite having read books with titles like 'How to listen so kids will talk, and talk so kids will listen'. I was all too aware of my inadequacies and failings. In a moment of such insecurity I welcomed hearing my friend Vimla say, 'You work harder than most women I know, yet you spend much more time with your children than women who are housewives.' I would not walk away from responsibility for my children and my choice meant learning how to balance everything that needed to be done. However, released of the expectations and frustrations of shared parenting, I experienced a new lease of energy. My children's insistence also helped me to focus on them and leave the day's frustrations behind. I revelled in the fun they created with their imaginations, despite the playground cruelty they experienced from other children as the new outsiders at school.

In Durban, Parusha and Yashodan had attended their fair share of meetings, rallies and demonstrations. Friends from UDW, where I had studied and then worked, recall me carrying one or the other on my shoulders during demonstrations. Several good comrades, contrary to their liberated political views, would insist that I was 'spoiling' my kids because I refused to beat them for 'naughtily' interrupting me while I talked to adults. Instead, I entertained their questions and observations, believing that children had the same right to respect as adults.

Parusha and Yashodan deepened my criticisms of what seemed standard union practice in those days. They would object to meetings filled with cigarette smoke where the only food comrades seemed to eat was good imperialist fare: Kentucky Fried Chicken

and Coke. Once, when Yashodan was three or four years old, he sat listening for ages to the speeches in Jayendra's union before piping up loudly, just as his father started to speak: 'This is so boring.' Parusha and I tried to shush him but he refused to pipe down. Yashodan unwittingly provided a pressure valve for the women workers who had been listening passively to the male leadership for hours. Insubordinate giggles broke out and took over as the women slapped their thighs and shook with laughter, the tears rolling down their faces.

Parenting was an area in which I learnt a lot about power, as I sifted through my recollections of what had nurtured me and what had undermined my potential as a child. Parents, like teachers, have enormous power to nurture or abuse the children they are responsible for. I learnt of important distinctions between punishment and discipline, as I tried to affirm positive behaviour without resorting to destructive criticism and corporal punishment.

It was not just the obvious wrongs that I tried not to repeat. I also had to confront and transform the subtle desire within myself to try to bend my children to my will, rather than allowing them to flow into their own unique sense of self and purpose. This took, and continues to take, a great deal of conscious attention and awareness. Having grown up in a racist, patriarchal and capitalist society, there were times when I naively assumed that I could somehow have escaped imbibing its prevailing values of fear, hate and greed. Yet I knew that conscious effort was (and is) required to transform myself. Parenting remains one of my most rigorous testing grounds. Amidst my failings, the understanding and practical skills I did develop proved integral to all my work, whether as a teacher or a trade unionist.

My children sustained my spirit in many ways. They helped me not just to survive but to keep joyful as I looked at the changing seasons through their eyes. The drive to my children's new school

went through a long, tree-lined road, over which the mountain rose like a vision. Parusha and Yashodan's delight in the changing colours of the leaves awakened me to the beauty of Cape Town's clearly demarcated seasons. Slowly I began to appreciate the early morning crispness and change of sky as the love affair with Cape Town that had started in childhood reawakened.

There were mornings, though, when Parusha despaired of both Yashodan and me, and our lack of punctuality; when the traffic seemed interminable and Yashodan's car, which would glide over all the traffic jams, had not yet made its way from his imagination to the road; when the day seemed too glorious to spend inside a classroom or, in my case, an office where I still experienced the fall-out from my role in Actwusa's 'defeat' at the inaugural congress. On one such day Yashodan quipped, 'Let's go to the beach instead.' It was enough to get me to turn the car around and head off to the sea, amid Parusha's protests, which ensured I never repeated this particular misdemeanour.

My union salary was meagre for a single parent. Materially it was a difficult period but Parusha and Yashodan seemed to enjoy eating vegetables and large amounts of fruit, which were cheap at the vegetable stalls in our neighbourhood. On all sides we were assailed by consumer culture. In the early years I had refused to buy a toy gun for Yashodan, who turned his fingers, pieces of paper, and bits of wood into guns. Parusha had received her first doll from one of our friends and I had acceded to her wish for a Barbie doll when she went through a short-lived, pink Barbie-doll phase. I slowly learnt to relax my concerns about my children being socialised into the omnipresent culture of the market. I learnt to trust my parenting and my children's own judgement.

Breakdancing had reached South Africa while we were still in Durban, and Yashodan hit the floor at home. He became the king of breakdance, dethroning Michael Jackson, his head and neck movements reminding me of the Indian dance moves that

I'd tried, and failed, to learn as a child. In Cape Town, as soon as I came home after work, Yashodan would insist I leave everything else, sit down with Parusha, and watch him breakdance.

After several months I switched schools and found a better one in which Parusha, during her first year there, won almost every prize in her class. In her reports, her teachers always said she was 'a pleasure to teach'. She won swimming races, loved netball, and her artwork captivated all of us. In high school she painted a picture, which today hangs in our home in Cape Town, of Yashodan and herself absorbed in playing with buckets of water on Durban's warm sunny beach. In adulthood, after finishing university, Parusha took a decision to work and travel by herself in different countries. I respected her courage in forging her own path in life but often missed her creative presence and had to learn how to let go. In between waitressing, Parusha taught in England and Venezuela, helped edit a children's magazine in London, and is honing her craft with a children's book publisher whilst freelancing for a year in South Africa.

Yashodan did not deploy his intelligence on schoolwork until he excelled in his final year, while organising a martial arts competition at the same time. In primary school and most of high school, his teachers all said the same thing: 'He would do excellently if he applied himself.' Well, he *was* applying himself. He was studying dinosaurs and investigating space travel through the universe. He wanted to be a palaeontologist. His piano teachers enthused about him: 'He has a natural talent. It is a rare and beautiful gift.' Yashodan stopped playing the piano as a teenager but returned to it as a young adult. Creating music became his life's passion as he applied the same inspired discipline that had turned him from a bullied, skinny boy into a muscular young man, who is gentle and kind to his little brother.

Today, Parusha and Yashodan joke that I was really a hermit and home with them was my cave. I knew that my yoga practice

helped me, most times, to shut out workday worries and listen to them. One of the big downsides of this, as Yashodan recently pointed out, was that they grew up aware of their mother's love as softness, at times even as weakness, which did not provide the clear direction they wanted. There were times when I thought that love meant I had to tolerate everything, even disrespectful behaviour. I sometimes confused the line between humility and self-esteem. Getting the balance right is an ongoing struggle. It is the same criticism that Daya, in a moment of disillusionment in his youth, once yelled at my father: 'It is a lie that the world operates on love – you get treated as a weakling and smashed if you believe that bullshit.' My young children were unaware of the difficult times in which I drew on love to cope with my own fear about the obstacles before me. Talking about these struggles might have helped me apply that same courage to more areas of my life than I managed. Perhaps it could also have reinforced the lesson that love, like gentleness or kindness, is not weakness.

In the Sactwu offices in Cape Town, despite the warmth I experienced from my old union comrades and from gentle women leaders like Frieda Henry, I felt the full impact of what Actwusa's general secretary meant when he'd said 'our guys will never forgive you for losing the election at congress'. His 'guy' in the Western Cape had a passionate commitment to the union that I deeply respected, but he exercised power in a very controlling fashion. I was confined to doing research on collective bargaining and could no longer spend time on any educational work. At this stage I enjoyed becoming part of the women's movement in the Western Cape with feminist comrades like Beattie Hofmeyr, Gertrude Fester and Lynne Brown, and enjoyed addressing some of the meetings they convened of the Women's Alliance. I was also appointed to a board that was set up by the vice-chancellor of

the University of Cape Town, Mamphela Ramphele, to oversee a project against sexual harassment. The board helped develop her proposal for an Africa-wide gender institute. Despite all this, I was frustrated at not being able to interact directly with shop stewards through education, the work I loved most of all.

It was during this time that the inspiration for developing a workers' college emerged. Both the trade union federation Cosatu and Sactwu, as an individual affiliate, had resolved to start one, but like countless other resolutions it had lain buried forever. What if I implemented the idea, created a space where workers learnt practical skills and acquired information on matters like political economy, collective bargaining, organisational management, international solidarity, and the rest? Surely this would strengthen them in grappling with power, equip them for leadership, and help build a culture free of racism and sexism.

It was not good enough just to criticise the way power and leadership were exercised by the enemy and within our own movement. We needed to develop our own alternative understanding and practice. Apartheid and capitalism had limited workers' choices at every level, including education. For most women workers, from morning to night, life was a backbreaking, soul-deadening grind. A workers' college could be a space to reclaim oneself in.

I went ahead, reaching out to opposing unions with the vision of what could be achieved together, developed funding proposals which secured the resources we needed, and helped negotiate a space at the University of the Western Cape. The Workers' College came into being, and it really did work as a place of renewal and empowerment. Rachel Visser was the first Workers' College student to be employed by Sactwu and it was not long before she was appointed as their national media officer. Recently we discussed her impressions of the college. We began with the poem she had written there. 'I remember that so well. You made us

relax our bodies, to breathe and let our minds open. It was the first time I'd relaxed like that – it was so peaceful and still in that room. Then you taught us to write poetry. Workers writing poetry! Oh, it was a beautiful experience.' Her poem described her walking into the college thinking she was ugly, useless, unintelligent, a poor parent. It ended on these lines: 'I walk out of the college and I say to myself: "Rachel, woman, you are beautiful, you are intelligent, you are an excellent parent."'

Another student at the college, Neville Alcock, quiet and wise, wrote: 'The Workers' College changed my perception of building power and how to use power. We must build power for the collective good, encourage individuals to develop and take responsibility for the running of our organisation – even if it means that those in power are sowing the seeds for others to take their place – we must not fear this.'

Our pilot course inspired a range of brilliant academics, activists and unionists to give their time and teach at the college free of charge. On the board, though, two men from opposite ends of the political spectrum behaved in a similarly destructive manner. They dragged out board meetings, squashing enthusiasm and alienating the goodwill on which the college had been built. One of these men was my nemesis from the Cape Town office of Sactwu, who asserted excessively petty control over every aspect of the running of the college. He tried to keep even my low salary from a basic increase, despite knowing that it was used to run a home and maintain two children. The other had gone around trying to drum up opposition to my appointment in the first instance, by telling comrades that I was not 'politically sussed'. Used to a tradition of labelling and dismissing viewpoints that differed from his own, he was critical of my attempts to ensure that the college encouraged debate of ideas across the political spectrum.

The independent evaluation of the board was a welcome contrast to the negativity spread about by the two men. Our pilot

course and my own role were endorsed, and the report (by Debbie Budlender of Case, the Community Agency for Social Enquiry) noted: 'There seems to be almost unanimous consensus that the first three-month pilot course of the College was a resounding success. The venture was not without problems. But most of the suggestions which I heard were on how to get *more* of what was already good, rather than on areas which should be removed.' The evaluation also noted that 'the co-ordinator had performed, with great charm, dedication, enthusiasm and hard work, an amazonian task ... [which] was also a draining and time-consuming one.'

The whole process had been very rewarding but had indeed taken a lot out of me. One of the ways I revived my energy was through dancing.

One warm Cape Town evening I went partying with my brother Pat and his wife. Several unionists from Durban, including Yusuf, were at the party. As our group made its way to the dance floor I greeted him cordially. Between dances Yusuf came up to me. 'Tell me something, Pregs. How can you look so happy after what we did to you? It was worse than what the cops did to us in detention.' But this was not the place for sombre talk. I laughed and replied, 'I do yoga, Yusuf. It develops the quality of bamboo – I bend but don't break.' It was a strange but important moment as Yusuf finally acknowledged the past. Around us, in the Cape of good wine and the tot system, glasses clinked, the music played, and people danced.

PART 3

Power

Twelve

SISTERHOOD

In 1990 after Mandela was released and political parties were unbanned, the ANC Women's League was re-established inside South Africa. Internal women's organisations like NOW dissolved. Their experience with the League was not sisterly; many described the encounter as a bruising process.

On their return from exile a number of ANC women, including Mavivi Myakayaka-Manzini, Brigitte Mabandla, Baleka Mbete, Thenjiwe Mtintso and Frene Ginwala, who had worked within the ANC in exile to advance debates on women's emancipation, described themselves in a magazine interview as feminists. Their decision to call themselves feminists, in the context of the times, was striking. Like all political parties, the ANC, despite its progressive gender policies, was still patriarchal in practice. When the ANC and South African Communist Party began serious negotiations with the National Party (NP) government, the two key negotiators, Cyril Ramaphosa from the ANC and Roelf Meyer from the NP, led almost entirely male teams. While this was expected of the NP, there were much higher expectations

of the ANC. In the 1991 talks at Codesa, the Convention for a Democratic South Africa, where the basic elements of the new South Africa were hammered out, the ANC had only 2 women out of its 20 delegates. Both women were called 'advisers' but had no speaking rights.

At the time, feminism was still highly contested territory. At one of the first United Nations women's conferences held in Nairobi, ANC women had fought and won against the liberal feminism of Maureen Reagan, who attempted to disconnect politics (and criticism of apartheid) from 'women's issues'. They refused to allow Maureen, daughter of US President Ronald Reagan, to colonise feminism. Like Britain's Margaret Thatcher, Ronald Reagan supported apartheid and denounced Mandela as a 'terrorist' who should remain incarcerated on Robben Island. Being a woman does not automatically mean opposing the authoritarianism of systems such as apartheid, capitalism or even patriarchy itself. Indeed, patriarchy could, and often did, appear in female guise, clothed in the most feminine and sometimes even feminist garb.

Within the feminist movement in South Africa, there were deep divisions and hostilities. These came to a head in 1991 at a gender conference at Natal University, which threatened to splinter into divisions between activists and academics and between black and white women academics. Over tea and lunch the frustrations burst out and a great deal of anger was expressed. The divides continued under the surface and threatened to tear us apart.

An inbuilt resistance to women talking about other women as stereotyped 'gossips' impels me to find ways to raise my criticisms openly and constructively. In the plenary I proposed that the organisers create space for women to air the problems and suggest solutions. This was agreed to and at 6 pm we broke into two formal caucuses, one for those who saw themselves as activists and another for those who wanted to caucus as black women. While I recognised the problem of race politics within the feminist

movement, I identified with the urgency of changing society encompassed by the word 'activist'. The activist group, of black and white women, was huge and we split up into smaller ones. At the end, I was given notes from the small groups to summarise and report back to plenary.

It was a long night as I read through the bits of paper and tried turning them into a constructive presentation. Activists were not anti-intellectual, as is often believed. They were engaged in and knew the value of intellectual work, and they articulated the problems sharply: 'We had expectations that a gender conference would be more sensitive to women; instead it is just a reproduction of conferences organised by patriarchal men.' 'Black women are the subject of white women academics' research.' 'White women are identified as the academics and black women are perceived as mindless activists.' 'Activist intellectuals are excluded from the programme.' 'The organisers and presenters of this conference are, shockingly, predominantly white.' 'Absence of black women academics.' 'The objectification of black women as data is considered normal.' '95% of white women studying blacks.' Despite the fears of some, airing the problems did not destroy the conference but instead enabled it to begin grappling with difficulties that still challenge the feminist movement.

Despite our differences, we often did manage to unite, act and change things. In April 1992, for the first time in South Africa's history, the broadest range of women's organisations joined forces in a new Women's National Coalition (WNC), an initiative of women in the ANC. Remarkably, the coalition united women across major divisions and endured even through the aftermath of the Boipatong massacre of innocent civilians, which threatened the negotiations for democracy. The coalition united women from opposing political parties, from the National Party to the Pan Africanist Congress, from the conservative Afrikaans organisation Dames Aktueel to the Communist Party. Frene Ginwala, who was

the driving force behind the coalition, was elected convener. In her speech Frene noted:

> Our experience has been that the more powerful the committee, the fewer the women. The exclusion of women in the Codesa process is both a symbol of our present society and a grim warning of the future. They will talk of non-sexism, they will not practise it. The air around us is thick with talk of change, of the end of racism and apartheid, of a new era of democracy. Is the change we are all talking about going to mean simply adding some black men where white men sat before?

Several months after the founding, Frene met me to discuss the coalition. A short, sari-clad woman with an impatient edge to her sharp intelligence, Frene was widely respected. She came straight to the point: she wanted me to head the coalition campaign for the Women's Charter. Would I apply for the job? It would not be easy. The ambitious objective was to have a massive participatory research campaign to persuade South African women to say what they wanted in the new South Africa. Like many of us, Frene was concerned about women being excluded from critical decision-making in Codesa and worried that valuable time had been lost. The coalition had been launched at the beginning of 1992, the end of the year was fast approaching, and it still had not been able to get the campaign off the ground.

Frene was charmingly persuasive. I became excited about the possibilities for strengthening the women's movement through the coalition. It was clear to me that unless women at the negotiating table were backed by a strong women's movement, they would not be taken seriously. They would be powerless to make the changes women needed in South Africa's new constitution.

When the post was advertised in the *Weekly Mail*, one of

the tasks listed was 'to co-ordinate and plan all aspects of the campaign'. I applied and went for an interview. In the interviews, the committee was assisted by a senior personnel officer from one of the big corporates. Months later, Frene told me that this woman had warned them that I had a mind of my own. Despite this, the coalition's steering committee appointed me. I felt inspired by this chance to make sure women's voices would be respected in a post-apartheid society.

But accepting the job was not an easy choice to make. I had to relocate to Johannesburg with my children, establish a new home for them and once again find a new school. It was a hard cost they had to bear but I weighed it up against the fact they would be able to spend more time with their father and their grandmother, Sanna, who had both been based in Johannesburg for a while. My children were not easily persuaded and I promised them that we would return within two years.

I did not underestimate the challenge that faced the coalition. Within the coalition a genial notion of sisterhood, a vague idealism, was not going to sustain us. Behind the rosy talk of the 'new South Africa', there were frightening realities to be faced: the high rate of unemployment, women's unpaid and unrecognised contribution to the economy, the divide between poor and rich, the continuing hidden violence especially against women and girls, the fact that the majority of rural dwellers were female.

Women had to start from this reality, recognise their own power and raise the debate in the country by putting women's issues on the agenda in all political parties, in trade unions, in sport, media, the law and education. It was up to each one of us individually and collectively to do this, and to make each other aware of what we could achieve when we came together. As women took action in different parts of the country, these experiences would build the campaign nationally. And so my mantra became: 'Use the coalition campaign as a catalyst to build women's power. Don't

expect power to come from up above, like manna from heaven.'

Right from the start there was a wonderful sense of possibility, in the national organisations, in the regions and among the new coalition staff. Debbie Budlender, the earnest-looking, hard-working and efficient researcher from Case, whom I had met through the Workers' College, applied for the post of research co-ordinator and was appointed. I looked forward to us working together. In the first few months the head office attracted several other talented women: Deborah Marakalala for media, Merle Caminsky for special events and education, Priscilla Pietersen for projects, Margaret Roper as office administrator, Thandeka Mali to co-ordinate the campaigns and Lilian Mokoa as secretary. Several others joined us over the next year, including volunteers like Gabrielle le Roux. I served on the working and steering committees as well as in the research and legal groups. The coalition brought together many brilliant South African women whom I enjoyed working with and learning from.

After my first few weeks of intense work in the coalition, I went out with good friends. The first party was clearly not for dancing but my friends Heather and Coralea quickly learnt of one with dancing in Bez Valley nearby. To tide me over till we got there, I reached for a handful of snacks. At that moment someone else did the same. I smiled at the beautiful eyes I saw. At the second party I danced till I was dehydrated. As I left the kitchen, I bumped into someone and spilt my full glass of water on him. I looked up to apologise and saw the same lovely eyes. We spent the rest of the party together and continued talking till the sun came up.

I am not sure exactly when I fell in love with Paul Benjamin – maybe over our long walks through the streets and koppies of Johannesburg or during slow dancing to Ella Fitzgerald singing Cole Porter. Paul's home was on the ridge overlooking Bez Valley

and he loved it. 'Close your eyes and listen – the traffic becomes the waves of an ocean.'

Paul is not one for talking much about himself. Slowly I learnt that his life had involved a hectic work schedule as the lawyer for the National Union of Mineworkers, where he handled South Africa's biggest strike of 350 000 mineworkers and worked trying to rectify the terrible lack of health and safety conditions in the mines. I discovered that he had a taste for fine music, books, movies and holidays in wild places. When we met each other's parents, we laughingly agreed that his background as a typical 'repressed Wasp', while mine as a typical 'passionate Indian', had left their mark. Perhaps our search for balance led us to each other and remains our challenge. Years later, Paul accompanied me to a state function, where I introduced him to the president of our new democracy. Madiba chuckled to him: 'You made a wise choice, heh heh! Or maybe she chose you.'

After a short while in Johannesburg I finally found a house near the school Parusha and Yashodan attended, and the three of us began our new life there. My parents visited and planted vegetables in my tiny back garden. For months after they left the garden continued producing spinach and massive tomatoes. I could not afford a washing machine but discovered a laundromat five roads away in Rockey Street, a hub of creative and social life. Feminists in the ANC and the Coalition – Feroza Adams, Baleka Mbete and Brigitte Mabandla – all lived close by and we spent some lovely relaxed evenings together, talking and laughing about our work and lives. Most of us were migrants in Johannesburg, so we shared an identity as transient workers.

In the coalition I proposed that we launch the Women's Charter campaign on International Women's Day, 8 March 1993. As in the Workers' College, a shoestring budget inspired creativity. My

friend Gcina Mhlophe, a renowned storyteller, led the event in her usual sparkling, wise way, Frene gave the keynote address, and I spoke about the campaign itself. The launch had the impact we'd hoped for, generating publicity that boosted South African women's issues. Well over half of South African voters are women, and the message in the media was that women were gearing up to use that power in the elections. The following month, women delegates to the Codesa negotiations at the World Trade Centre won an important victory. The political parties and organisations gathered there agreed to their demand that each group should include an extra woman delegate. Women at the World Trade Centre were no longer standing alone.

Inside the coalition, however, a key cause of the initial delay in getting the Women's Charter campaign off the ground was becoming clearer to me. There was a problem within the coalition's own leadership, involving the convener, a woman I deeply respect but whose leadership style is very different from mine. Frene Ginwala's strengths are legend. She was able, for example, to get the male leadership of the ANC to listen to women's demands. However, it was her key weakness, reflected in an abrasive management style that impeded the development of the campaign. Unfortunately this is the dominant leadership style in many organisations, including the ANC, despite the model provided by leaders like Walter Sisulu, whose sharp intellect was accompanied by a gentle, encouraging manner. It was difficult to confront the problem but inevitable that I should. It is not easy to tackle feminist sisters because the patriarchal system we are all up against is powerfully oppressive and divisive. Every one of us internalises this mindset and we have to consciously act against replicating it ourselves, especially in relation to those over whom we hold power.

The coalition steering committee included many people from very small constituencies. Some effectively represented themselves,

such as a non-governmental organisation (NGO) that consisted of two members. The organisations that were disproportionately represented were mainly white and upper or middle class. As the person entrusted with the campaign, I believed that the women at whom the campaign was largely aimed had to be involved from the start. One of the first things I did was to contact the Cosatu national women's committee in which I had worked. The women on it had experience of conducting large campaigns with a massive signed-up membership. I also wanted to visit the regions, both to help women initiate regional coalitions where none existed and also to hear how women at grass roots wanted the campaign shaped. Frene vehemently opposed my meeting with Cosatu, arguing that it was not strategic. But despite Frene's objections, I did meet with Cosatu women. From the start, I also attended workshops in every region across the country, beginning with a vibrant one in the Eastern Cape, organised by feminist Thoko Matshe, who became a close friend.

In my first few months at head office, I watched, dismayed, as Frene's manner impacted on members of the working committee and staff. It was easier to understand why the liberal and conservative women were unnerved: few came from a tradition of challenging the authoritarianism they encountered in their homes, communities or organisations, and they crumbled when they met it in the coalition. But even seasoned comrades suffered.

I began to comprehend the paralysis that had stultified the coalition since its inspired formation in early 1992, beyond the obvious difficulties of its disparate membership and organisational structure which made decision-making difficult. One of the first casualties of the unhappy situation was Debbie Budlender, who resigned in frustration. Her leaving made me act faster, as I realised that I had been rendered powerless to protect those for whom I was initially given responsibility. I knew that one of the ways to maintain my enthusiasm was to keep a clear focus on my purpose in

joining the coalition and actively seek those who had such clarity. One of those who helped me do so, without even being aware of it, was Mam Lydia Ngwenya. It was a relief to work with her in the coalition. She was intent on advancing the interests of rural women and was not engaged in the power plays of the coalition. We had first met when I was at the Workers' College and we had both received Ashoka fellowships in recognition of our work. A veteran of the Transport and General Workers' Union, she had founded the Rural Women's Movement, one of the groups that succeeded in keeping the area of Moutse from being incorporated into the bantustan of KwaNdebele even when the apartheid government cut off Moutse's water supply. During the Codesa negotiations, these rural women successfully mobilised against traditional leaders who had attempted to exempt customary law from the Constitution's commitment to gender equality.

Mam Lydia and I were invited to address the annual general meeting of the Southern African Methodist manyano (mothers' union) on the subject of the coalition's campaign. Organisations such as the manyanos and stokvels (savings clubs) formed the real backbone of the coalition and it was important to participate in their meetings. I drove us through dusty roads to get to the church in a Bloemfontein township. The manyanos, whose rallying point is their faith, form one of the largest and best-organised constituencies of women in South Africa. In our first few minutes there the women slammed the coalition as 'political' – and, worse, as 'supporting abortion'. They told us that they were 'church women who pray and wait for things'. 'We ask nicely; we don't demand like political women.' They argued that the 'role for manyanos was to pray and to pray and to pray'. Righteous voices rang out against abortion and its evils. Scripture was quoted eloquently, and often, by the women in their neat red and white uniforms.

Fortunately, an elder stood up and reminded the congregation, 'We invited them to come and explain things to us. We should give

our guests a chance to talk and hear what they have to say instead of just attacking them.' Mam Lydia spoke first. She was angry at the attacks but angrier at the views that had been expressed. We did not speak for long – we were both used to getting straight to the point. Between the two of us we clarified that the coalition was formed to unify women across a wide spectrum so that their voices were heard in the constitution-making processes to ensure real equality for women. The Women's Charter would declare the rights that women wanted. We explained that women across South Africa should use the campaign to identify their issues and exercise their power.

We didn't duck the issue of abortion they had raised. We both agreed that this was not an easy decision. Every single woman in that church knew the pain, shame and stigma attached to abortion, we said, whether for ourselves or for a mother, daughter, sister or neighbour. Though the Nationalist government had legalised abortion under limited circumstances in 1973, those who could access this right were mainly wealthy white women. Most black South African women had no recourse to legal abortion and suffered serious damage or death from 'backstreet abortions', with an average of 400 women dying every year and an estimated 20 000 more being hospitalised for serious injuries.

At the meeting something finally shifted. An elder of the church came forward. 'They are right. Jesus spoke of compassion. We must show the same compassion. It is time to follow His example.' Others, including those who had damned abortion before, sat quietly, wiping away tears. Despite their rhetoric, they knew the truth of women's experience – now they wanted to know about their rights and the role of the coalition. The person chairing it declared that 'women can no longer run from politics' and urged the congregation to join the coalition, to put forward their views and demands. Later that year the Methodist manyanos participated in the coalition's national council.

During this time, there were one-day workshops in every region around the country. Cities like Durban, Cape Town and Johannesburg had long had women's organisations and were the homes of well-known feminists, so although I attended and spoke at their workshops, I didn't need to prioritise them. Instead I made sure I focused my energy on those in rural areas like the Eastern Cape Border region, where women travelled long hours to reach the workshops, determined to make their voices heard. They were not the passive objects of someone else's research – they were claiming their own agency to act to change their lives. The campaign acted as a catalyst, enabling women living in rural villages to unite amongst themselves against apartheid and patriarchal chiefs. They voiced their concerns with a sense of power, a confidence that they were not isolated but belonged to a national movement of women.

One of the big challenges was to integrate the two key objectives of the coalition's campaign, by ensuring that the research for the Women's Charter campaign was conducted in as participatory a manner as possible. The conflict with Frene had heightened and I knew that if I presented any plan to try to move us forward it would be shot down. In a moment of inspiration, I developed a plan of how we could do the research in the most participatory manner, wrote it up and ran it by Paul, whose quiet intelligence I deeply respect. The coalition needed a combination of research strategies co-ordinated around the practical issues that confronted women. I knew that opposition to the plan would be neutralised if it came from someone in the research supervisory committee and asked Paul to drive me to Sheila Meintjes's home. Sheila, a political scientist at the University of the Witwatersrand, was a key person on the committee. I took her through the plan and she agreed to develop it further and present it to the coalition's steering

committee. The next day the plan was unanimously adopted.

Another major hurdle was our funding. Our main donor had suspended its funding to the coalition as a result of the impasse signalled by Debbie Budlender's resignation as research co-ordinator. Rosina Wiltshire, a Caribbean feminist, was sent by the donor to evaluate the coalition and recommend whether its suspension should be lifted. Rosina needed to see that the coalition was capable of achieving its objective of empowering women through its participatory research campaign. I worked with our research committee on plans to hold a workshop to develop research skills in women from the regions. Our treasurer, however, refused to fund it, insisting that it was too great a risk to take. In my view the workshop was the only way we could break the logjam. I finally told the treasurer that I would pay the costs myself if the workshop failed to convince the donor, but she needed to release the funds immediately. It was a risk – I had very little money in the bank and had taken out a mortgage for my home – but there didn't seem any other way.

At the workshop Rosina sat quietly, observing. I had never met her before. At tea she asked, 'So, what *did* you do there this morning?' I was nervous and explained about the ice-breaker and the team-building exercises. 'No,' she responded impatiently. 'What did you really do there? I have never seen energy being released like that before.' I was silent, not knowing how to answer her question. She scrutinised me and a broad smile broke through, like the proverbial cat who has found the cream. 'You meditate, don't you?' I relaxed. This was someone who was familiar with meditation. In my activism, I did not discuss meditation. Yet I knew there was nothing complicated about it. Meditation was that silent time, after I dropped Parusha and Yashodan at school and before heading into the office, when I focused on experiencing the inner power of peace, joy and love. In such silence, I saw the deeply engraved patterns of self-negation, yet was able to trust the

clarity that emerged. Meditation also enabled me to listen with deep recognition and respect for the gifts others had to share. I did not know how to explain this in the coalition's workshop, but with Rosina's intuitive intelligence words were unnecessary. 'If you can release that kind of energy in even ten women, the coalition will certainly receive our funding,' she said happily.

Of course that was not all that Rosina did. In her thorough evaluation she talked to many others in the coalition and scrutinised our research proposals and capacity. The result was that the coalition secured its funding. Years later, when Rosina and I had become friends, she invited me to stay at her flat in New York. As the sun rose, I went into her lounge to sit in silence and saw her already in meditation, her small upright body seated on a tiny wooden bench on her veranda.

After our successful research workshop, important organisational steps had to be finalised. I had argued that if women identified at least five issues in the regional coalition workshops, we could use these to build the campaign. We asked the ninety national organisations affiliated to the coalition to do the same. To consolidate the five issues, I planned a national workshop, which the head office team worked hard and well towards.

Just before the workshop I received a call, asking me to cancel it. I was tired of being told to conceive and write up the campaign at my desk in the coalition office on the 36th floor of the Carlton Centre. Long before Debbie's resignation, the two of us had produced draft after draft, in a circular process that had gone nowhere. I believed that the workshop would ensure ownership of the campaign by women on the ground, and would give the coalition the boost of energy it needed. I listened politely to Frene's order and her ultimatum that proceeding with the workshop would cost me my job. But on 12 June 1993 the workshop went ahead as planned and women from every regional coalition finalised the five issues: legal status, land, violence, health and work. The campaign

finally rolled out across the country. Women were creative in how they used the resources put together in the coalition national office. They organised and mobilised around the issues, uniting and supporting each other while collecting demands for the Women's Charter. It was a wonderfully focused period. Even Frene, to my great delight and relief, seemed to be infused with enthusiasm for what was unfolding.

The teams of women researchers co-ordinated by Stoncey Lebethe, our dedicated new researcher, found the research easier to conduct as the campaign finally began to cohere. From July to November the five issues were used to collect valuable information. We had a tight schedule but the issues provided a clear framework for women in both the national organisations and regional coalitions to raise their specific concerns. The campaign urged women to speak out about all the issues that concerned them, including violence against women, to get their stories into the media and make the public aware. Some journalists could not understand my insistence that we were there to connect them to the women who were taking action on farms and on the streets. A journalist, angered by my refusal to be personally profiled, retorted, 'How can you run such a public campaign and no one knows who you are?' But this focus paid off. A media firm that had monitored the campaign later said that, in the period of our work, coverage of women's issues in hard news went up from about nothing to almost daily mention. An estimated two million women, we were told, had participated in the campaign.

In November 1993 the Interim Constitution for a new South Africa was negotiated into being, and women's rights were integrated into it in a way that few constitutions in the world had managed to achieve. It was thanks to a powerful movement of women across South Africa mobilised behind skilled negotiators like Frene, Brigitte, Baleka, Thenjiwe and Mavivi that women's interests were secured in our Constitution.

Shortly before the conference to round up the coalition campaign in February 1994, I left for my short but eventful trip to India. On my return, I found a very efficient staff member uncharacteristically tearful and a bundle of nerves: in my absence she had been undermined to the point where she now described herself as 'useless'. By the end of our discussion she decided to focus on what had to be done to finalise the conference, as we were literally two weeks away from completing the work we had set out to do.

That night I knew that it was time to move on from the coalition. My contract had expired in October the year before and had not been renewed but I had been too focused on completing the job I had committed to, to pursue it with the person in charge of contracts. But my job was now complete and all that was left was the national conference. At the conference women from across the country came together to finalise the Women's Charter. Thanks to the coalition's campaign, many women pledged themselves to using their access and power to ensure that women's voices were never silenced again.

I handed over my letter of resignation to the general secretary, Thoko Msane, explaining that it was effective from the end of the month but that I would stay on for a few days to tie up loose ends. The letter was clear about why I was going. 'I believe there is a place for each of us but that cannot happen if we do not respect each other as women. I came into the coalition and moved to Joburg because I believed in a vision of what the coalition could achieve. I remained because of that and to complete the task given to me – that is now complete.' I also faxed Debbie a letter, telling her of my resignation and thanking her for laying the ground for the campaign's research.

One of my last duties was handing over the coalition campaign report to Madiba, as part of the coalition's delegation. It was the first

time I would meet Madiba, a real privilege. I do not deify Mandela, who, aware of his fallibility, often pokes fun at himself. But my experience in India made me realise how much I had benefited from his leadership. In attempting to live by spiritual values, I was sometimes deeply hurt by the actions of people grasping for personal or political power. Madiba's humanity in the face of personal and political pain was reassuring. When he was released from Robben Island, he insisted on speaking only the best of De Klerk, despite the fact that De Klerk had presided over terrible state-driven violence in apartheid's last years. Madiba's hurt and anger at De Klerk's betrayal of trust with the Boipatong massacre was palpable. Madiba had battled with the spiritual imperative of love that looks for the highest potential in every human being. He had elevated De Klerk to a Nobel Prize-winner and had been met in Boipatong by cynical real politik. Yet Mandela did not himself become a cynic.

The night before the meeting, I was as excited as a small child. I wanted nothing more than to sit quietly in Madiba's presence for even a few minutes. But on the morning of our visit I had a phone call informing me that I had been excluded from the delegation. For the first time in the coalition, I argued for what I wanted for myself, not just as an advocate for or representative of other women. I insisted that I could not be excluded. Fortunately, Thoko agreed that as the person who had managed the campaign I should participate in the culmination of our work.

When we met Madiba, I was tongue-tied. I did not expect him to know who I was and was overwhelmed when he not only knew my name but also acknowledged my contribution. He held my hands, smiled warmly into my eyes and sent my heart soaring.

Standing up for what you believe can lead to being written out, not just out of history but out of herstory, not just by men but by women. The coalition was not the first nor the last lesson in understanding how easy it is for women to internalise the

dominant understanding and practice of power and leadership, whether it manifests itself in lack of respect for other women or in the way those of us who stand up against such disrespect face the possibility of being erased. Nevertheless, these consequences did not diminish my own respect for the women I had worked with, including Frene. I knew that without her role in initiating the Women's National Coalition, it would never have existed and I would not have had the opportunity of sharing such a unique moment in 'herstory'.

Thirteen

IN MANDELA'S PARLIAMENT

In February 1994 I was nominated for inclusion on the ANC's list of candidates for parliament. I felt ambivalent. But three friends and comrades, on their way back from the final list conference, sat down gleefully in my kitchen and announced: 'Now you have no choice. Cosatu's women workers have put you on the list. You'd better go to parliament and represent them well!' Shortly afterwards a progressive journal quoted me as saying optimistically that we would 'go into the existing power structure and transform it'.

In the month before the elections to parliament I worked in the national Reconstruction and Development Programme (RDP) office in Cosatu, believing that the RDP would help the new government address poverty and redistribution. The tripartite alliance of the ANC, Cosatu and the Communist Party was firmly united on the platform of the RDP, whose four goals were building the economy, meeting basic needs, developing human resources, and democratising the state. But as I read through the RDP drafts, I realised that the work that women in the alliance had done

to ensure the RDP was a gender-sensitive document had been completely ignored.

With the text so close to being published, it was not an ideal time to intervene – I had always argued against 'adding on gender' – but women's experience and proposals simply could not be omitted from such an influential document. Although I was not on the team of editors, I asked if I could do a 'gender edit' and Cosatu's general secretary, Jay Naidoo, who was in charge of the RDP office, agreed. However, any changes had to be in the following day, when Alec Erwin, who was one of the editors, would have the last word.

That night, when Parusha and Yashodan were fast asleep, I began my work. I used the report of proposals from an ANC-led workshop on women and the RDP as the basis for my edit and carefully found ways to reinsert women's analysis, recommendations and proposals. I was surprised when Alec accepted several of the changes. Some, including one on the provision of shelters, were rejected. Still, I knew that those changes which were accepted – such as 'A key focus throughout the RDP is on ensuring a full and equal role for women in every aspect of our economy and society' – could be usefully built on in the future.

We were constructing our dreams for the future in a violent time. I remember going to ANC headquarters, then called Shell House, for a meeting with deputy secretary-general Cheryl Carolus, on the RDP, when tens of thousands of IFP supporters, carrying traditional weapons, marched into town on 28 March. I had been in the foyer, signing in, when someone shouted, 'Hit the ground. They are shooting at us.' It was a terrifying moment. Later I was in my office, when news came that the IFP were marching to Cosatu House. We were all ordered to remain inside Cosatu House. I called a friend to fetch my children from school and take them

to Sanna but one of Cosatu's administrators didn't know anyone who could collect her children from their crèche, which was along the route that the IFP were taking. Despite the order, I took her to fetch them. While she was inside, the IFP marched past and I scrunched down into my seat, my heart thumping furiously. By the end of that day, 53 people were dead and 250 had been admitted to hospital for serious injuries.

On 27 April 1994, I stood in a queue with my father and my old comrade from NOW, Thoko Msane, waiting to cast our votes for the first time, with millions of South Africans across the country. We laughed a lot that day, slightly disbelieving perhaps that our country, after all the death and suffering that had gone before, had finally reached this point.

After the ANC's overwhelming victory in the elections, all MPs were flown to parliament for the first time. The night before, Paul had a farewell party at his house. The next morning I woke with only a few minutes to spare to get to the airport. I showered quickly and plonked the black bowler hat I had been wearing the night before, onto my unwashed hair. I raced to the airport where I joined hundreds of MPs, including many legendary figures, who spent hours waiting to be 'processed'. In Cape Town, we were taken from the airport. For most of us the drive through the gates of parliament was our first time there. The décor inside ranged from institutional green to shiny kitsch marble. In these buildings, decisions had been made that had meant misery and death for many South Africans. Those responsible – the old white men, many now dead – loomed over us in huge photographs along the corridors and even in the dining-room. Now we were to take over control and accountability, sitting where they had in the Assembly, a large airless room with no natural light or air, ventilated by freezing-cold air-conditioning.

When we came to be photographed for our ID security cards, I discovered that I was listed under my ex-husband's surname. When I married, I had gone through a lengthy process with the Department of Indian Affairs to keep my surname. Yet his surname continued to pop up, first on the electoral list and then on parliament's roll. I asked an Afrikaner MP, Jannie Momberg, who had been in the NP and was now in the ANC and in charge that day, how I could correct the error. He thought it was hugely funny and refused to take my request seriously until I lost my temper. By the time we took our oaths as MPs my surname was reinstated.

Paul and I had decided to buy a house in Cape Town. At the first opportunity we took Parusha and Yashodan house-hunting but it was a tiring business and soon the children were only too glad to leave the job to us. After we'd seen several areas, I wanted to look at a house in Pinelands. Paul objected. 'That's an area full of ex-Rhodesians and old white pensioners who worked for Old Mutual,' he said. It also smacked far too much of suburbia for a man who had lived life as a bohemian bachelor.

Still arguing, we turned into a wrong road and I spotted a house for sale. The small cottage looked welcoming and I fell in love with it. Its outside appearance was misleading. Once inside, I relished the prospect of opening up the wonderful space by removing the thick brocade curtains and heavy furniture that filled it up. We fetched Parusha, Yashodan and their cousin Kamil, who raced about the house and gave it their firm approval.

The next day I told the lawyer who was trying to secure my divorce that I could provide a home in Cape Town for my children, an issue till then in contention with my ex-husband. After I had sued for divorce, he had counter-sued for split custody, which literally entails one child to each parent. For me this reduced our children to material property. For months I woke at dawn to

meditate so as to keep my clarity and my children together. The order finalising our divorce was formalised by the court in August 1994. In the early hours of dawn and late at night, before and after parliament and while the children were asleep, I celebrated by replanting the English garden of our new home with indigenous Cape plants. Perhaps all this internal work released the raw energy with which I tackled my new job as an MP. Paul returned from negotiating a convention on mining health and safety at the International Labour Organisation and began helping government draft laws such as the Basic Conditions of Employment Act. In our new home, with Parusha and Yashodan, we began the slow process of creating a family and a life together.

At President Mandela's inauguration in Pretoria, Paul and I watched the ceremonial flypast by fighter planes. Two MPs behind us joined in the crowd's spontaneous, exuberant whistling, cheering and clapping. 'They're ours now!' Ronnie Kasrils and Phillip Dexter laughed triumphantly, a boyish glint in their eyes. It had been a long, difficult road to that moment. Ronnie, a pleasant-looking bear of a man with big, bushy eyebrows, was about to be appointed deputy minister of defence in Madiba's cabinet after his contribution to the ANC's armed struggle. Although I knew that for many the military display represented our newly acquired ownership of power, I still felt uncomfortable with the centrality of boys' war-toys at such a significant moment.

In the first ANC caucus, all of us women voted for Frene Ginwala to become Speaker of South Africa's new parliament. In the most powerful seat in the National Assembly, she was a powerful symbol – a woman in a sari, not a suit. A significant change was being signalled, considering that everything in the Assembly was filtered through systems established long before, using language and symbols that seemed to belong to some ancient

phallic cult: MPs were 'members'; an important symbol was the 'staff', a rod; the first speech was a 'maiden' speech. The day we were sworn in, the service officer guarding the entrance insisted that I walk upstairs to the 'wives' gallery', where he thought I belonged. He courteously invited Paul, who looked more the part, into the National Assembly.

For the swearing-in ceremony I wore a simple white cotton kurta that I'd bought on my trip to India for the equivalent of R10, a colourful scarf, and a pair of leather sandals. It was a relief to see that I was not the only one who had dismissed the attempt at a women's workshop we all attended to have us change the way we dressed and talked to conform to this very British institution. Gill Marcus wore her usual kaftan and many MPs donned traditional outfits. There were of course the conventional European hats and suits, not just among the opposition but in our own ranks.

I sat on the back bench next to Lindiwe Sisulu, one of the smartest MPs, whose intelligence was rightfully recognised and rewarded with a cabinet post. On our first day, she drew a big smiling face on a blank sheet of paper. 'We love you, Madiba,' she wrote next to it and passed it to me with an impish grin. 'Go, on, sign it.' One of the service officers took the note to Mandela and I craned my neck to watch our president read the note. He turned round, looked at both of us, grinned and waved – I was in love, along with millions of others! Later, as Paul and I drove back home in the returning traffic, my old Volkswagen, which I'd had since my days in Durban, broke down on the busy highway. I think it was the first time that an MP stood there hitching a lift. Fortunately we were quickly helped by a comrade who recognised me and pulled over.

In the Government of National Unity, former NP leaders and many rank-and-file members of their bureaucracy retained their old positions. A joke favoured by male friends, quoting American president Lyndon Johnson, was that 'it was better to have them

inside pissing out than outside pissing in'. Considering that they had designed the House with so many urinals, they should have had enough practice, in either direction. Almost all the toilets in parliament were designed for men. On the floor where my office was located there were two toilets, both for men. On my first day I took a large piece of paper, wrote in big, bold letters 'Women's Toilet', and stuck it on one of the doors, ensuring an equitable redistribution of services. Later I discovered a very smart toilet with pink chairs and a large lit-up mirror for 'MPs' wives'. Quick-thinking Lindiwe, with her usual sense of style, swapped the drab green chairs in her office for the pretty pink ones. It was not just the toilets that were designed for men: there were men's-only gyms, subsidised pubs, not to mention the long hours and the way the Assembly conducted itself with a pugnacious debating and heckling style.

Apartheid's parliament, established by white Afrikaner men, reflected their traditions, norms and values. The long-established institutional culture did not prize African women veterans such as Albertina Sisulu and Dorothy Nyembe who brought a wealth of experience with them. Instead, their contribution was wasted and buried under often meaningless mounds of paper and procedures. Many MPs, especially the elderly and those not literate in English, battled to cope with the huge piles of documents in English and Afrikaans that landed on our desks every morning. Parliament had no proper research and secretarial services to help separate what was useless from what was worthwhile. Like most others in the ANC, I initially shared the services of a secretary with over sixty other MPs. The veterans expressed a growing lack of confidence. For them, parliament seemed to be a place for lawyers and businessmen. Many of us were flooded with invitations from businessmen and diplomats. I decided to decline them in favour of invitations from women's organisations and poor communities. There was only so much time and I had to prioritise it if I was to contribute anything of value.

Many opposition MPs strolled into parliament in the afternoon after having spent their mornings managing their farms and businesses. For them, parliament was a part-time job. The pubs were particularly busy in the afternoons and evenings, when voting compelled everyone to stay in the building. After a late start, there would be two hours of much state-subsidised eating of greasy meat and mayonnaise-drenched salads in up-market dining-rooms. This was followed by long tea breaks filled with fresh cream cakes and greasy pastries. I began to understand the reason for the girth of apartheid's MPs like Pik Botha and realised that we would quickly join them if we weren't careful.

As a result of the 30 per cent quota for women on the ANC's list of parliamentary candidates, which ANC women had secured, South Africa could boast one of the largest numbers of women parliamentarians in the world. While the ideal was for men and women to share responsibility for housework and childcare, the reality was that most women still bore the load. Those who did not could generally afford not to. A woman MP from the Democratic Party responded with ridicule when I asked how she'd managed to balance family and work in the old parliament. A woman of 'old wealth' with several servants caring for her home and children, she sneered at what she saw as my stupidity: 'You just have to be organised!' Most men, whatever their party, seemed happy to respond *ad hoc* to crises rather than develop long-term plans. They could do this because most of them had women as wives, nannies and domestic workers to take care of children and domestic work. The wages many MPs paid their workers was appalling, as was evident when a basic minimum wage for domestic workers was introduced and some MPs, across political parties, were quoted in the media, arguing that they could not afford to pay more than R500 a month (while we earned around R20 000 a month). I saw no reason why parliament could not plan its work within a clear timetable so that we could all contribute effectively while leading

more balanced lives. We surely could not provide compassionate leadership for our country if we did not exercise such leadership over ourselves and in our homes.

Many men in parliament joked that the women could not keep pace, but the truth was that most women often had to work much harder. While many of us could now afford to (and did) employ domestic workers or childminders, we still had to balance the parliamentary schedule with fair employment practice. Jenny Schreiner, one of the few feminists in the SACP and my neighbour on the back bench, provided a good example, when she left promptly at five in the afternoon to relieve her childminder and take care of her five-year-old. Wisely, she didn't wait for the arduous decision-making processes which depended on ever-fluctuating political will. Many of the women started working early in the morning and tried to finish at five. They usually worked a full, far more productive day than the men from the old apartheid parliament, who seemed to conduct much of their business in the pubs and the dining-rooms. At lunchtimes, instead of tucking into a huge meal in the dining-room, Jenny joined me for the yoga class I organised with 70-year-old Ivan Agherdien in the gym. Over the next few years ANC women MPs caucused and changed the toilets, the all-male gyms, the working hours and secured a parliamentary crèche. These were important victories, although such changes needed to be formalised in order to be sustained, and many were not.

Our democratic government inherited many things from apartheid including the draft report to the United Nations conference on women in Beijing. I was asked by the RDP office in the Presidency if I would read and correct the report. Among several omissions, the report ignored the former homeland areas and, hence, one-fifth of black women in South Africa. It reflected how invisible black women's lives were to apartheid bureaucrats. My criticisms led to my being tasked with editing our country report on the status of women in time for the Beijing conference.

I approached Debbie Budlender from Case and Nozizwe Madlala-Routledge, my old comrade from NOW who was also an MP, to work with me on the report. We combined our skills and completely transformed the report. The new one was launched by the minister of water affairs, Kader Asmal. Respected as a feminist thinker within the ANC, he applauded the report for its 'activist, campaigning' style, which would 'hopefully convey the urgency of the real issues to those who have become absorbed by bureaucracy and protocol'.

Geraldine Fraser-Moleketi, the minister of social development, led the national preparatory committee for Beijing after Sankie Mthembu had set it up, and I worked with both of them on this body. In government's first two years Geraldine had responsibility for co-ordinating gender equality issues. She convened workshops on establishing mechanisms to promote gender equality, such as the Commission on Gender Equality. Through these workshops I developed respect for her willingness to listen and act and was disappointed when a man who did not share her understanding or commitment was appointed minister in charge of the status of women.

It was Geraldine's unfortunate role, as minister of welfare, to introduce the reformed Child Care Grant. This piece of legislation took from the poor to give to the poor. Social security benefits were now being characterised as 'hand-outs'. When we debated the childcare grant, Clinton's stereotype of the single mother 'on welfare', the source of all society's problems, was quoted repeatedly. Geraldine was lampooned as 'Geraldine Thatcher', despite the fact that budget decisions are the result of economic choices driven by cabinet and the treasury, not individual ministers. Without denying a leader's responsibility for his or her choices, Geraldine's experience illustrates why it is necessary not just to vote women into positions of power but to change the priorities of the institutions themselves.

It was clear that government needed a coherent women's national empowerment policy to guide the work of all its departments. This was one of our major recommendations in the Beijing report. I proposed to the RDP ministry that they should try to implement it. Jay Naidoo, the RDP minister, Nozizwe Madlala-Routledge, who was now chairing the ANC women's caucus, and I formed a task team. I drafted something on the framework for the policy and gave it to Nozi, who added her changes and passed it on to Jay. Several talented women including Mmatshilo Motsei, who had founded the first organisation to work with survivors and perpetrators of gender-based violence in Alexandra Township, were employed by the RDP office to develop the policy further through consultative workshops. Our collective work helped lay the basis for South Africa's national gender policy.

Fourteen

PARLIAMENT'S ENGINE ROOMS

The main work of parliament was and is conducted largely through its committees. The National Assembly is mistakenly depicted as parliament's engine room. From our first year as MPs I had found the Assembly to be a 'schoolboy's debating society of hot air and rhetoric', and characterised it as such in my 'maiden' speech. In the years since then, little happened to change that initial impression and television-viewers continue to see MPs snoring in their seats. In 1994, the ANC deployed me to several committees, including the RDP committee and the finance committee.

I argued with Feroza Adams when she told me of my deployment to the latter. 'But I am not an economist!'

'Ja, we know that, but we want you to go there and do what you do best – protect and advance women's interests.'

'Be realistic. I'm an English teacher who has taught in the union movement. Teaching political economy in the unions is not enough preparation for the finance committee. I'll be out of my depth.'

'Listen, Pregs, no one here has done any of this before and all of us have to learn new things fast. You can do it.'

Few of us in the finance committee were economists. Fortunately, our chair, Gill Marcus, and Barbara Hogan, who convened the budget working group, arranged an intensive ANC study-group programme to equip all of us with much more than the rudimentary knowledge. Over the next few years economists like Rob Davies, Ben Turok and Max Sisulu (who also chaired the RDP committee) organised seminars where we met a range of progressive economists (none of whom were feminist).

Through the finance committee I learnt how significant sections of white business had benefited from their special access to and collaboration with the apartheid government. One example of this is that during apartheid, over half of the department of trade and industry's budget went to subsidising large white-owned companies through the 'general export incentive subsidy scheme'. On the day of the Budget, business would also host the finance minister at a special breakfast briefing on the Budget. Business was accustomed to wining and dining apartheid MPs, treating them to overseas holidays and expensive gifts. In return, the old MPs sorted out anything that obstructed the smooth functioning of business or did what was required to promote it. There was no code of conduct whereby MPs had to declare gifts; no conflict of interest was registered; and corruption was not investigated or charged. This was just the way things were done. Business assumed that after 1994 it would continue to operate as it had done in the past.

When the Truth and Reconciliation Commission held its hearings into the role of business in apartheid South Africa, many felt angry that these players escaped scot-free despite having benefited from apartheid policy. Paul, who had helped draft Cosatu's TRC submission, came home angry. Mine-owners had not taken responsibility for the huge number of deaths from occupational accidents underground and diseases like HIV/Aids; they had not done much to change the underground conditions that caused accidents; and they had not addressed changing the

single-sex hostels that exacerbated the spread of HIV/Aids. Those who were seriously injured or became too ill were sent back home where they died, miserably poor. Like many other ANC MPs, I assumed that my party, now in power, would transform this situation so that the concerns of the poor were at the top of our agenda. Though the ANC did initiate anti-corruption legislation and put in place ethical codes of conduct for MPs, transformation would not be as simple as I had assumed.

In the first hearings of the finance committee, the director-general of state expenditure, Hannes Smit, disparaged the questions I raised. 'The finance committee, Ms Govender, deals with macroeconomic issues. Questions on women's issues and poverty must be directed to committees such as health or welfare.' He smiled as if explaining what was surely obvious even to the idiot he was addressing. I was angry, but persisted in asking the questions no one else was raising. Slowly but surely, other members of the committee began supporting me in viewing the economy from a gender perspective. A few years down the line, Hannes himself shifted his position and he was once even introduced in our committee hearings by the finance minister Trevor Manuel as 'our gender specialist'.

Opposition to seeing economic issues through a 'gender lens' came not only from the old guard but also from erstwhile comrades. Competing loyalties were a source of tension from our very first year in parliament. There was pressure for us to slot uncritically into the global order. Many leading ANC economists were invited to attend courses devised by institutions and think-tanks in the United States that promoted capitalism. It was not just the ANC that such prestigious 'think-tanks' sought to win over; they reached out to journalists, political analysts and leaders in civil society. As part of a global economy led by institutions such as the World Trade Organisation, we were now expected to prioritise the rights of corporations above the rights of people. This undermined

the human rights and gender equality we had entrenched in our Constitution. The global trend was for 'leaner government' and the privatisation of basic needs such as water, despite privatised water being unaffordable for poor people. Such privatisation meant that poor women spent hours trying to find free, clean water and even more hours looking after family members when unaffordable sanitation led to the spread of water-borne disease and epidemics like cholera. I knew that transforming an institution built on the values of greed, accumulation and the self-interest of those who still retained control of the economy would be difficult. What I had not realised was how quickly we too would be absorbed by the same values and priorities.

When the finance committee planned its hearings on the Budget, I proposed that we examine its impact on the poor and on women. There were hoots of ridicule. Though the response from the opposition was predictable, I was surprised by the voices from our own benches. 'Poverty hearings on the Budget? Come on, Pregs, we're dealing with macroeconomic issues here' was the comment from a former trade union colleague, visibly irritated. (It was not too many years before he left concerns of poverty behind him to pursue the task of becoming a multi-millionaire.) Fortunately, another ANC MP, Rob Davies, a professor of economics and a communist, led the argument in support of the hearings. Several other ANC MPs, including Gill Marcus in the chair, agreed. From then on, it became standard practice for the finance committee to scrutinise the Budget's impact on poverty and on the people who formed the majority of the poor, women and girls.

When the head of Statistics South Africa came before the finance committee, he agreed that women could not remain invisible and that his unit needed to track just whose lives were changing and how. He also agreed that Stats SA needed to count and value women's often unpaid contribution to society, such as subsistence farming. In the conventional analysis, growth,

as reflected by gross domestic product, measured increased production, whether of guns or armoured vehicles, so countries at war could theoretically have a higher growth rate than countries at peace, because economists seldom measured the everyday work of maintaining peace.

On International Women's Day in 1996, I moved a resolution in the Assembly, calling for gender-disaggregated data and performance monitoring. Maria Ramos, director-general of the finance ministry, addressed these issues in an amendment to her minister's speech, which she ran by me, before inserting it. The minister's speech was a statement of political will. Not long afterwards Stats SA began collecting gender-disaggregated data for the first time.

The most contentious statistics which emerged from Stats SA were those on rape. During apartheid, when police used violence to protect apartheid and had a reputation as perpetrators of rape, most women did not feel free to report rape or any other acts of violence to them. In the Women's Coalition campaign we encouraged women to break the silence on rape and report incidents to the police. In our new democracy, large numbers of women began reporting for the first time, trusting that their rights would be protected by those they had voted into power. As the new government began collecting the statistics of rape reports, people were shocked. As part of the global economy South Africa had become prey to one of the most lucrative trades: global crime syndicates who trafficked in women and children for sexual exploitation. Our record as a post-war country was horrifically compounded. A few years later, the FBI announced that South Africa had the highest rate of *reported* rape in the world, which some carelessly abbreviated to 'the highest rate of rape in the world'.

The erroneous reporting of the FBI's statement became legend in the United States, itself a place of endemic violence against

women. Many there believed that, along with lions roaming our streets, misogyny existed only in deepest Africa, instead of being the tragically shared global culture that it is. After 1994 many apartheid-era politicians smugly implied that black majority rule equalled violence against women, almost as if they were presenting themselves as our new liberators. My feeling was that we had to address this violence in South Africa and in our world, not as some point-scoring exercise but for the real crisis it represented.

In 1996 Frene Ginwala, as Speaker, set up an *ad hoc* committee on the improvement of the quality of life and status of women, which eventually became a standing committee. I was elected to chair it. Our brief was to monitor the way the government implemented its commitments to the United Nations Convention on the Elimination of all Forms of Discrimination against Women and the Beijing Platform for Action. A large number of ANC women veterans, like Ellen Kuzwayo and Mittah Seperepere, consistently attended the meetings, even though some of them were not formal members of the committee. Their involvement and supportive presence lent a quiet power to our work. We were fortunate that so many of the most powerful ANC women, old and young, worked in the committee at one time or another.

Our priorities in changing the law followed on from the demands that women across South Africa had made during the Women's Coalition campaign before the 1994 elections. The first major victory for women came in 1996, with the law on reproductive choice, which ensured the right of access by all women to abortion, not just white privileged women who had been the primary beneficiaries of apartheid's abortion law passed two decades earlier. Our law was vociferously opposed by conservative religious groups inside South Africa as well as by the Pope and Mother Teresa, whose attacks on our law were read out at Catholic

schools, including the one my children were attending. Right-wing churches in the United States poured money into attempts to stop the law, as gruesome pictures were emailed to MPs. In the debate on the Act, my speech, which argued for reproductive choice, proposed that this had to be accompanied by expanding political, economic and social choices. There was a standing ovation from the Assembly and, significantly, from many in the gallery who had been demonstrating against the law. Several analysts saw this moment as a turning point. For me, the most treasured comment came from my mother, who had watched the debate on television in Durban and phoned to thank me, for 'speaking for her'.

In the year of our committee's formation we talked to many women's organisations and invited them to parliament to present their experience to our hearings. The relationship we built with them was invaluable in drawing up our legislative priorities. We sought improvements in the Child Maintenance Act, the revision of customary law as it related to marriages, inheritance and succession, and new laws on domestic violence and sexual offences. We also proposed that labour laws should address maternity rights, child care, sexual harassment and other concerns as part of improving conditions in the workplace. We wanted to do away with women's minority status especially under customary marriages, abolish the marital power of husbands as guardians, and ensure that wives became equal to their husbands in status. Women needed equal decision-making power, including the right to enter into contracts, to own land and to inherit property.

But it was not easy trying to get agreement that women's issues should be prioritised by the ANC and parliament. The committee found itself on the wrong side of powerful people in the party hierarchy. Attempting to have the priorities taken seriously by the justice committee, I met with its powerful chair, who shouted, 'To hell with this! We've got other priorities! Since when are women's laws the priority?' He was not the only one to have responded

in this way. The chief whip of the safety and security committee reacted in an even more aggressive manner to our later attempt to influence the Firearms Control Bill. We had intervened to support submissions from lobby groups who argued against guns, for gender equality and for children's rights. Despite such reactions, I persisted, knowing that the year before the general elections was a good time to push for the changes that women wanted.

In our effort to get women's legislative priorities onto the agenda, a meeting with Deputy President Thabo Mbeki played a critical role. About eight women from the ANC women's caucus met him at his home to discuss the party's approach to gender-based violence. We were also concerned that within the ANC there was no disciplinary procedure in cases of rape or sexual abuse and no dedicated committee in place to deal with them. One of the cases raised was the rape of Nomboniso Gasa on Robben Island in 1997. After her assault she took a courageous decision to speak out about her experience, including the appalling bungling by the police and authorities involved. Nomboniso's response eventually benefited many other women as important reforms were recommended by the Independent Complaints Directorate on how the police needed to treat rape survivors and improve investigative procedures. Most rape survivors do not report their rape, and even fewer are prepared to speak publicly about it, as women who speak out are stigmatised as hysterical, neurotic or insane.

At some point in our meeting Mbeki chided us. 'You ANC women need to get your act together.' I had brought a list of priorities in my bag, hoping for a chance to raise them, and saw his statement as the ideal opportunity to intervene. I presented the priorities to Mbeki as an example of how ANC women often *do* get their act together but lack the power and access to crucial structures such as cabinet to ensure things are taken further. He was silent as he accepted the piece of paper and so was everyone else in the room.

When we left, there was none of the usual chit-chat after a gathering. The following week a senior woman comrade informed me that Mbeki had convened a meeting of senior staff in his office and told them to move on our committee's priorities. At the same time an acquaintance in the South African Law Commission asked what we had done, because suddenly it was apparent in the commission that strong political will was being asserted. Having the priorities taken seriously at such a high level was bound to have an impact. The chair of the justice committee, in his typical hard-working style, buckled down and played an important role in holding the necessary hearings. By the end of 1999, Madiba's parliament had enacted about 80 per cent of our committee's transformative legislative priorities for women. They included the Domestic Violence Act, the Child Maintenance Act, the Customary Law on Marriages Act, and changes that benefited women workers in the labour laws. Still, parliament's engine rooms needed a captain at its helm to support bills that were against the tide. Instead, two key priorities for women, the bills on Sexual Offences and the Customary Bill on Inheritance and Succession, were sunk and only began to re-emerge in 2007.

THE WOMEN'S BUDGET

A gender-sensitive Constitution, policies and laws were important but needed substantial resources to implement and impact positively on women's lives. While questioning the finance minister and his director-general in committee in 1994, I searched for a practical way to ensure that economics would address the desperate reality of poor women. Late one night, I turned to some bulky files sitting on my desk. Nozizwe Madlala-Routledge, who had worked for the Transitional Executive Committee (TEC) sub-council on the status of women, had passed them on to me. Buried in this forgotten mass of paper I found proposals on gender, economics and budgets that several feminist economists had compiled. They included a two-page summary of the Australian Women's Budget Statement, an initiative which Australian women had begun almost a decade before, but which had not since been used to influence a national budget in any other country.

In parliament's Budget debate in 1994 I proposed that the finance minister use the TEC's gender checklist of questions on income and expenditure when working on future Budgets. I also

suggested that he scrutinise a range of other areas for their impact on women; 'for example, the free-trade zones, the International Monetary Fund and structural adjustment policies, privatisation, trade liberalisation and deregulation'. The challenge, I said, was for government departments to set goals that were measurable, realistic and within clear time frames.

My proposal that South Africa should develop its own Women's Budget won an immediate response from the minister, Chris Liebenberg, laying the ground for the practical commitment towards the Women's Budget that his successor, Trevor Manuel, made a few years later. As Frene Ginwala said afterwards of my intervention:

> It was very, very crucial because, for the very first time, during the parliamentary debate new issues were being raised. I am not sure if it was the shock or the revelation. However, for a member of parliament from the ANC to be questioning an ANC budget and get support was crucial. It was done very positively. It brought an almost immediate response, though the minister of finance did not come from the same party. That was a very important thing in that it was right at the beginning, right up-front and it did not allow for a pattern to be set because changes were signalled.

The timing was crucial. We had come into parliament on the back of a powerful women's movement, which created the space to push the boundaries in the interests of poor women. But it was a space that would not last too long. In 1994, insubordinate women had not only been elected to parliament in defiance of the truism that 'women's place' is in the kitchen and the bedroom, but were also presumptuous enough to talk of a Women's Budget. The words 'women' and 'budget' clanged against each other and the audacious phrase captured attention. We explained that the

Women's Budget was not a separate budget for women. It was, in fact, far worse! It was a way of analysing the entire budget for its gendered impact on women, who were mainly poor.

As a member of the ruling party and as chair of a parliamentary committee, I had access to structures of power that few others had and did not hesitate to use my position and access to advocate the Women's Budget. If the powerful participants at most of these forums were convinced of the value of a gender analysis of budgets, they could make a difference to the average citizen, who was not a middle-class white man in the formal economy, as apartheid budgets had implied, but a poor black woman. Once they saw that economics and budgets were not gender-neutral, those with power could influence the budgets of national departments, provinces and local governments and bring about significant changes in women's lives.

The fundamental component was building political support for the Women's Budget. Women needed to build political power to secure political will. Locally and internationally, legislatures, government departments and civil society needed to challenge their own organisations and governments by using the Women's Budget, for it to contribute to change. Many of us worked hard to spread the word. For myself, over the next few years, in meetings from townships to United Nations conferences, I tried to pass on the idea and inspire others to do the same.

One such meeting was the ANC's cadre development summit in 1996, at which most of the participants were men in key leadership positions. I felt nervous and needed to take a deep breath before stepping up to the podium to explain why economic policy should be scrutinised from a gender perspective. There were many examples, from countries across the globe, of what happens if policy is made by someone who ignores gender. One of the worst I'd heard of was a maternity clinic built on top of a hill, which provided good advertisement for the donors, but

was useless to the pregnant women who could not climb to the top, when they needed to give birth. Gender budgeting required long-term planning based on the reality of existing gender roles, relationships and power. For instance, instead of responding to crime by simply building more prisons, resources would be spent on building community infrastructure (including houses, libraries and children's playgrounds), creating viable employment and investing in education (from crèches to adult education). I hoped that the summit's powerful participants would be persuaded to use their power to make a difference to women's lives. They included finance minister Trevor Manuel, Gauteng minister for finance Jabu Moleketi and Maria Ramos, all of whom did go on to play a major role in institutionalising the Women's Budget, before conservative economic policy took hold.

A meeting that proved significant in creating international momentum behind the idea of gender budgeting also took place in 1996. The Association for Women's Rights in Development (AWID), at that point probably the biggest international network of feminists, held a massive meeting after the United Nations conference in Beijing. In its plenary session, I listened closely to the other panelists. Vandana Shiva, a scientist, talked about international trade rules that disadvantage small women farmers. She revealed how US companies sought to patent seeds and traditional remedies. Using the example of turmeric, which has anti-inflammatory properties, she explained that patenting would mean poor women being banned from using their own traditional remedy unless they bought the patented, packaged version at high cost.

After her, Diane Elson, an economist, talked about the 'care economy': the work most women do in bringing up children and caring for family members who are sick, disabled or old. She showed how women bear the fallout, the 'hidden costs', from conservative macroeconomic policy. It was then my turn to share South Africa's

Women's Budget. I began with an exercise on power that illustrated the need to work with deep respect for ourselves and others: the power of love and courage. After my speech there was silence before the room erupted. Joanna Kerr, AWID's president, described that moment as the spark that inspired feminists internationally to use the Women's Budget.

Within parliament the process of actually realising the Women's Budget involved slow but steady advances. In the first years in the finance committee, we divided ourselves into small working groups to give in-depth focus to various policy issues. In 1994 I convened a group on gender and economic policy, which Beatrice Marshoff and Elizabeth Thabethe joined. Beatrice today is premier of the Free State and Elizabeth is now deputy minister of trade and industry. Ours was the smallest working group. Men in the committee took some time to be persuaded that it was an important issue – unlike the chair, Gill Marcus, who with Barbara Hogan supported our work on the Women's Budget. Women were entering a terrain that few of us had previously engaged with and we were refusing to accept that only the rich and powerful could make such decisions. In the women's committee's first set of hearings on poverty, economics and the Budget in 1997, economists and activists like Zanele Mbeki, Vivienne Taylor and Neva Makgetla-Seidman made presentations, one of the most striking of which was the critique of South Africa's new macro-economic policy. There were women who would not be silent on issues which impacted negatively on the lives of most women.

The proposal I had made in the 1994 Budget debate required us to analyse the existing policy underlying budget choices as well as propose alternatives. Researchers in South Africa and elsewhere had been analysing policy from a gender perspective for years, but their work had not been applied to budgets. In 1995, with two NGOs and our parliamentary committee we formed the Women's Budget Initiative. I nominated Debbie Budlender, whom I had

worked extensively with, as research editor. Over the next few years a number of skilled researchers analysed the budgets of every national government department as well as some provincial and local departments, using the TEC checklist of questions I had raised in the Budget debate as a guideline. Debbie, meticulous as ever, co-ordinated and edited this research, which was published as the *Women's Budget Books*. Many of the MPs and ministers who received copies commented that this research provided a helpful illustration of what a gender analysis of budgets entailed.

In Australia, the Women's Budget had been driven by 'femocrats' (feminist bureaucrats) through the office on the status of women located in the prime minister's office. In South Africa, two parliamentary committees tried to ensure the same result. Our committees exercised their duty to interrogate the executive as well as propose innovative solutions. Parliament provided very little research capacity to committees, unlike the United States Congress, for example, where every public representative has about 20 full-time staff, including researchers, journalists and lawyers. Our committee was fortunate to have its own researcher, Coriaan de Villiers, for about two years while we dealt with the priority laws. By forming the Women's Budget Initiative we were able to draw on the research skills of women in civil society, who appreciated the fact that we did not let their research gather dust on shelves. Parliament, first through the finance committee and then the committee on women, used its power to ensure that government institutionalised a gender analysis in the national Budget.

Already in 1997 we could measure the success of our project by the reception it received from finance minister Trevor Manuel. In a written report to our committee he noted that subsequent to my presentation on gender, macroeconomics and poverty at his conference on the medium-term economic framework, his ministry had committed to 'integrating gender analysis into macroeconomic

policy'. On another occasion, the minister explained that while they were committed to the Women's Budget, they did not have the funds for the work that was needed.

Later that same year a small team of us participated in the Commonwealth ministers' meeting in Trinidad and Tobago. Our delegation was led by the minister of social development, Geraldine Fraser-Moleketi, and I was invited to present our South African Women's Budget to the ministers. Before the meeting began, we had a caucus of our delegation. To my surprise, one of the women I'd worked with closely harangued me, asking me not to 'play your games, as these are ministers, not trade unionists'. She was referring to the adult education exercises I used to demonstrate the kind of power and leadership necessary for the success of the Women's Budget. Conducting such exercises was premised on respecting participants, whether ministers or unionists. In the room everyone else, including the minister, was silent. Perhaps they were as shocked as I was by my comrade's outburst. At the ministers' meeting, I made my presentation and then invited the ministers to 'play a game'. In a subsequent meeting in Sweden, my comrade presented the Women's Budget. A delegate from the Trinidad and Tobago meeting, after questioning my absence in Sweden, commented that he had never understood power as well as he did after 'that game'. The Women's Budget, like everything else, was unfortunately not always fun and games.

During the meeting in Trinidad and Tobago I battled with the flu and felt in dire need of a break. Our delegation was due to take the long flight back on Saturday and most wanted to rest. I wanted to see, smell and taste something of the beauty of the island. On Friday afternoon one of the other delegates, Colleen Lowe-Morne, joined me in hiring a small second-hand car. We drove out exploring the island, getting lost and stopping every short while to get directions from people who were extremely friendly to us. We eventually reached a magical beach and walked into

the rain forest next to it, becoming caught in a wild thunderstorm on the way back. At the small, simple hotel on the edge of the beach, we discovered that the woman running it remembered me from my speech in India in 1994. Warm and welcoming, she made me a ginger tea and honey for my flu. I woke the next morning completely refreshed. Before the sun rose, I was on the beach for a solitary yoga session and a swim, in time to meet up with Colleen for breakfast. We joined a young teenager on his boat around the little harbour while he fished. For lunch that day we ate the fish, freshly caught and cooked, at our hotel. It was only a few hours that we were away for, but it felt as if I had had a long, long holiday before our flight back home.

As a result of the ministers' meeting in Trinidad, South Africa was chosen as one of the countries that received Commonwealth funding for a pilot project to integrate gender into the national Budget. The collective work of our delegation paid off and the finance minister could no longer say that his department did not have the necessary funds. The work of women from parliament, government and civil society together made the difference. In the 1998 Budget the government made a pledge to 'integrate gender analysis into budgetary processes'. The Budget included 'gender-disaggregated information where available and appropriate, to permit an informed analysis of the impact of the Budget on men and women'. A good example of what this meant for women was contained in the Department of Water Affair's report. 'The Water Act specifies that a third of all members of Water Services Committees should be women. The Working for Water programme commitments include: ensuring that at least 60% of all salaries and wages should be paid to women, about 67% of the work should be in rural areas, and that single parents should be targeted with a policy of flexible time applied for those with additional responsibilities. In the first quarter of 1998, of 42 000 jobs created, 55% went to women.'

Applying a gender analysis to policy had potentially far-reaching consequences. Our committee worked with women in civil society and government to ensure similar analysis was applied to other important documents such as the Job Summit Agreement of 1998. In local, provincial and national government, as well as civil society, women used gender-budgeting to try to make women's rights concrete. To date, over seventy other countries have used the lessons from South Africa's Women's Budget. Unfortunately only a handful of these initiatives have had an impact on their governments' budgets. One of the reasons for this is that the Women's Budget is diluted into a technical tool by many governments, who then untruthfully claim that they are improving women's lives. The state of politics also often confounds budget initiatives, as happened in Sri Lanka, where the government, while being accused of atrocities in which women were being raped and killed, welcomed donors working on the Women's Budget.

Another factor in the lack of impact is that, globally, decision-making has shifted to unelected, unrepresentative institutions which protect the interests of capital above human rights. At the same time, more women have been elected onto representative institutions such as parliament than ever before. There they are confronted by conservative macroeconomic policy, trade agreements and patents that undermine women's rights. In South Africa the national Budget has ended its 1998/99 commitment to the Women's Budget.

Sixteen

MINISTER IN CHARGE OF THE STATUS OF WOMEN

Ideally, what would a minister in charge of the status of women in South Africa need to know? She or he should have a clear understanding of why women and girls form the majority of the poorest and bear the brunt of violence and HIV/Aids in South Africa – beyond the prevailing stereotypes that women and girls are inherently stupid, weak or ignorant. The minister would understand that gender, as socially prescribed roles and relationships of men and women, is a construct of power. She or he would see how gender intersects with class, race and other factors so those with least access to resources, status and opportunities are generally female. The minister would understand that if the yardstick of change was those at the very bottom, there could be a real possibility of changing the lives of everyone. She or he would grasp the challenges faced by half of humanity, would have a deep commitment to changing them, and would respect women's agency and power in developing solutions – in short, she or he would be a South African feminist.

The minister appointed was not a feminist. Moreover, the

original idea of an office on the status of women at the highest level of government was abandoned for a low-level office on women, alongside similar offices on youth and the disabled. All were placed under one minister. Many of us disagreed with the sectoral approach as it ignored the fact that amongst both the youth and the disabled, those who were often invisible, yet experienced the worst difficulties, were female. The sectoral approach often ends up pitting oppressed groups against each other in competition for pathetic resources. In the end the office on the status of women, while it was established within the President's Office, had little status, authority, resources or power. Oversight of this office and of the minister in charge of it fell to the committee on the quality of life and status of women. Ministers can frustrate committees by not appearing before them or by using their power to block access to information needed for evaluating government's work. On the other hand, ministers who appreciate the role of oversight can use the process to strengthen government's objectives, for instance, in delivering services.

The person appointed as minister in charge of the status of women, the youth and the disabled was Essop Pahad. He is a close friend of President Mbeki's, from their student days together at Sussex University. His membership of the ANC dates back to his youth and those who know him well say he has a good sense of humour. Unfortunately, from the very first year our committee was formed, in 1996, the minister and I began having major disagreements.

In that year, on the night before the debate on the adoption of the new Growth, Employment and Redistribution strategy (Gear), Lechesa Tsenoli, a member of the RDP committee, brought a copy of the policy document to my home. He had been in the lengthy and, I assumed, difficult meeting with leaders of government to discuss the launch. Few if any ANC members had had previous sight of the policy document, which many came to criticise as

embodying neo-liberal economic thinking. Lechesa was clearly tired. I did not ask him what the discussions were like and what his own opinion was, although his expression provided a fairly accurate summary.

Lechesa told me I had been chosen as the ANC speaker on behalf of women for the debate the following morning. I was expected to say why this economic policy was good for women. It was the first time I had seen it, and I told Lechesa I would only confirm speaking in the debate after I had read the document.

I couldn't understand the secrecy and lack of debate surrounding Gear. If the ANC caucus had had a chance to read and discuss this major policy shift, the difficulties which followed would have been significantly lessened. The first ANC caucus was full of talented, experienced members, several of whom worked on the ANC's economic committee. Many of them would have applied their minds to help develop an economic policy that truly would have strengthened the Reconstruction and Development Programme, creating employment and eradicating poverty. Instead, government's economic policy was drafted by a team of almost all white men, many of them consultants to the World Bank or IMF, organisations serving other interests than those of sovereign states like our own. As it was, the RDP office was unceremoniously shut down, the minister redeployed, and the RDP replaced by Gear.

When Lechesa left, I began reading through the document, relying on what I had learnt in the finance committee and through other lessons along the way. One lesson was never to speak on something you'd not had a chance to study in detail. Once, I foolishly agreed to speak on Tim Modise's talk-show on a Budget day. None of us had had a real chance to study the massive document we'd received that morning, and I should never have agreed to take part. All I could say to most of Tim's questions was that I couldn't comment, and still needed time to study the Budget properly. Never again!

So, the night before Gear's launch, I slowly worked my way through the policy, trying to see what it would mean for poor women. Gear aimed at 'a faster fiscal deficit reduction programme … a reduction in tariffs … tax incentives to stimulate investment … an expansion of trade and investment flows in Southern Africa … flexibility within the collective bargaining system'. It promised a great deal: 'a growth rate of 6 per cent per annum and job creation of 400 000 per annum by the year 2000.'

There were many puzzles. What cuts would result in a 'faster fiscal deficit reduction', and would the rich or would the poor carry this burden? What would 'flexibility' entail, especially for women workers?

At five the next morning I finally stood up from my desk. As I showered and dressed, I knew I would not stand on the podium and say that this economic policy was good for women, especially women who were poor. I arrived early in the National Assembly and told Lechesa I would not speak in the debate. Although I had said clearly that I would only confirm speaking after reading Gear, my name was already on the speakers' list. It had to be removed quickly or I would be called to the podium, but Lechesa explained that Minister Pahad was the only one who had the authority to change the list.

Even though I am tall, Essop Pahad is much taller than me, and as he looked down at me I felt uncomfortable. I explained politely that I needed him to remove me from the list. He responded with his usual charm: 'Hey *wena*, the ANC has chosen you as the woman to talk on Gear – that's a big thing, ja. It shows what confidence we have in you. Look at all the TV cameras being set up' – he gestured upward – 'the eyes of the world are on this debate.' I needed to keep focused as I engaged him. 'Comrade Pahad, I cannot speak in this debate on behalf of women on Gear. It would be best if you could find a replacement for me.' He exploded so loudly that MPs on the back bench heard him shout 'You are being politically

irresponsible', before he stormed off.

I was glad that I did not allow myself to be pressurised that day into saying that the new economic policy was good for women. The truth is that Gear's target of 400 000 new jobs per annum by 2000 has, till now in 2007, not been met. The jobs that have been created have been mainly in low-paid, vulnerable and unprotected work, and the numbers of jobs created do not match the increase in the labour force. The result is that unemployment levels as well as the numbers of the 'working poor', particularly women, have increased substantially and South Africa has one of the world's highest unemployment rates. Gear is often defended by shifting the blame to 'capacity'. 'Money is not the problem. The problem is capacity to spend the money.' The commonsense logic of spending money to develop the necessary capacity seems to escape those who articulate this line.

My next rough encounter with the minister was on the Women's Budget. As minister in charge of women he must have known that it was essential to re-prioritise how government collected and spent its money if we were to change the status of women. Yet he seemed oblivious of or opposed to the impact we were having with the Women's Budget, and its implications for women.

He launched an attack in an ANC study group meeting at his home. 'Women's Budget, Women's Budget ... you have spent years talking about something no one understands, you're just wasting all our time,' he shouted at me. I knew that the draft national gender policy, of which he now had charge, had deleted all reference to the Women's Budget and to the committee on women, despite the effectiveness of both. In the meeting, I steadfastly refused to be derailed by this emotional outburst and continued raising the issues we had come to see him about. I had spent years trying to learn how to stay centred and 'meet both praise and insult with equanimity' – although I know it's something I need to practise for the rest of my life. The minister tested me to the limit that day but

I was pleased that I kept a clear focus on our agenda and was not distracted into a slanging match.

But we couldn't afford to let him get away with such disrespect either. Later in an open public committee meeting when he shouted at rural women MPs, insisting that they knew nothing about the rural areas, I quickly called him to order. Rural women MPs such as Mam Lydia, founder of the Rural Women's Movement and now an influential member of the committee, were bringing crucial experience, insights and priorities into our policy debates. As a committee, we pushed to bring their wisdom home and were successful in ensuring that the minority status of women married under customary law was abolished. It was an uphill battle – women in rural areas bore the brunt of unjust apartheid policies and customary practice around ownership and inheritance of land and housing. They needed a minister who would advance their rights, not undermine their leaders.

PART 4

Choices

Seventeen

ELIMINATION

It was 1999, the end of the first term of South Africa's first democratically elected parliament. I stood outside the office of a prominent cabinet minister.

The minister had spent years on Robben Island in the close company of Nelson Mandela and Walter Sisulu. I was in awe of him and his experience, his long and courageous contribution to the struggle against apartheid. I had come to ask him about the underground unit in which Ahmed had appointed himself my commissar, on the day that he had brought me his fax, containing information that could only have come from London. As I waited for the minister, the childhood shyness that had made me stammer through primary school crept back. It sat in my throat, constricting it.

The minister was friendly in a formal way as he welcomed me into his office. He smiled as he gestured towards a sofa for me, and sat down on an armchair to my left.

'Yes,' he said, 'I knew that you worked with Ahmed. I knew about your unit.' He proceeded to tell me about his relationship

with my commissar in the ANC's underground. He had some fond memories of Ahmed, and also some difficult ones. He told me how he had worked closely with Ahmed on secret trips into the country during the latter years of apartheid. There was no mistaking the sense of camaraderie in the stories.

I needed him to verify the truth of my memories and listened intently. Had the minister known that I had asked – attempted several times – to be released from the unit? I did not describe the experience of those years in detail, but from the first I had not wanted to be in the unit with my commissar. I had, early on, reported the problems in the unit with Ahmed, to a trade unionist who had been released from Robben Island and was active in the Natal Indian Congress. His response had been that he could not intervene as Ahmed was the most senior person in intelligence in Natal.

The minister looked straight past me as he answered, keeping his gaze averted. 'Ahmed came to me and asked permission to have a woman comrade he worked with eliminated. I asked him, "Does she work for the state? Is she giving information to apartheid agents?" He said no. "Then why?" "Because she is insubordinate." "No! That is no reason to eliminate anyone, absolutely not," I told him.' The minister was emphatic, authoritative, in the way he recalled his refusal.

I felt cold. I cannot remember the rest of our conversation, the niceties we ended with. That night, after Parusha and Yashodan had gone to sleep, I cried as I shared my conversation with Paul. Afterwards I did not sleep at all. My mind kept returning to Ahmed and his request for 'elimination'. Ahmed was a senior ANC intelligence operative, respected by many within the leadership of the ANC's intelligence sector, despite the problems that several rank-and-file members had raised about him. An influential man, Ahmed's word was taken seriously. I wondered what would have happened if the minister had given Ahmed

permission to eliminate an 'insubordinate woman' at a time when it was difficult to guard against the abuse of power within our own ranks both inside the country and in exile.

We were fighting apartheid, a system so evil it had been denounced as a crime against humanity. In the face of such an enemy, what space existed to challenge hate and fear when it infiltrated our hearts, when we ourselves began to speak the language of 'elimination'? Apartheid had wreaked terrible damage. It had imprisoned the highest numbers of children in the world, some younger than ten years old. In apartheid prisons, many children and young people were tortured and raped, by warders and fellow prisoners. Those not killed emerged deeply wounded, silent about the visible and invisible wounds.

What happened to liberation movements forced to work covertly, to rely on information provided through networks that were subject to infiltration? What were the checks and balances to power in a time of dangerous secrecy and silence? What were the safeguards within our movement to ensure that those entrusted with power did not abuse it? What space existed to acknowledge and heal damaging wounds in a society where courage was defined by those who died for all of us?

The abuse of power had terrible consequences, some of which have now come to light. The ANC intellectual Pallo Jordan was detained in an ANC detention camp by his own comrades. The brother of Judge Pius Langa and Mandla Langa, Ben Langa, was killed when someone in ANC intelligence falsely alleged he was an informer and others colluded in the lie. Then there were those who had not been killed. Some of these survivors had been so badly damaged that they repeated the abuse of power in their treatment of others. There were unspoken destinies of 'insubordinate' women and girls whose names no one remembers and whose fate is not recorded. Misogyny, the hatred of the female, crushed and killed insubordinate women and 'girly' boys and men.

What terror led beloved friends, family and comrades to emulate the torturer in prisons, in homes, in organisations? What enabled others, facing the same terror, to commit themselves to using power with love and courage, to resolve never to repeat the fear and hate rained down upon them? How do some hearts remain safe from the brutality that demanded final victory?

On the next day, the last day of Madiba's parliament, there was an air of celebration in the National Assembly. I watched out for the minister, who entered with a jaunty air. As he made his way to his seat, I summoned the courage to go up to him. 'Thank you for what you shared with me. I cannot explain what it meant to me,' I said hurriedly. He was gracious, kind, as he gave me a comradely hug. I felt gratitude for life, for moments of truth which rip open my heart to pain kept quiet, hidden from sight for fear it will dissolve me. Then I tentatively touch it and realise that I swam safely through.

> Find the peace amidst the madness
> It's like finding hope through all this sadness
> This world is fuelled by so much anger
> As we swim against this tide
> > – 'Soldier', a song written by my son Yashodan

Eighteen

RIDING OUT THE STORM

In the morning after my meeting with the minister, I lit a candle and sat in silence, contemplating life. Paul, Parusha and Yashodan were still fast sleep. In the darkness even the birds were silent. In the early hours, life slowly filled me with its gentle, graceful touch. Orange light streaked across the sky as I unrolled my yoga mat and began stretching and breathing into the 'sun salutation'.

It was not long before my family unfurled from their beds – the sound of a toilet flushing brought me out of my corpse pose. I put my favourite pot of oats on the stove and ground cardamom into it, while warming a little oil. In the bathroom, the warm oil slowly lifted the panic that had covered my bones in the minister's office. Under the shower, warm water and soap cleared the film of oil. The sari I chose that day belonged to my grandmother, and then my mother. A sari of insubordinate women, it is brightly alive, in hues of peacock yellow and deep sea-blue. As I draped it over myself, its soft silkiness enveloped me.

The journey to parliament took me onto De Waal Drive. As I wound my way along the mountain, exuberance tinged with

hysteria coursed through my veins. I felt wildly, joyfully alive, despite the minister's frightening disclosure. In 1994 I had felt a distinct ambivalence about formal political power and being a parliamentarian. Yet in Madiba's parliament I had enjoyed working closely with other insubordinate women of the ANC to push the boundaries of policy and institutional change. I sat through the final farewell to our first president with a deep sense of appreciation for life. When we all stood to sing our national anthem, 'Nkosi Sikelel' iAfrika', I raised my fist in the air as the words reverberated through me.

After the adjournment there was jubilation and, of course, photos. The first, for me, were outside my office, with Phumelela Nzimande, a comrade I'd known since our days in the Natal Organisation of Women. In the picture we're laughing, happy as we hug each other. Later that night, at a parliamentary party in a big white tent at Fernwood, I took photographs of many of the ANC women I had worked with in South Africa's first parliament. I was laughing again, not caring what anyone thought of me as I tried, and failed, to get the prized photo with Madiba. Long after most others quietly retired for the night, I danced and danced with Paul, laughing … alive.

A few days later, on one of our energetic climbs into the forest on the side of Table Mountain, Paul and I returned to the question that generally found us on different tracks: Should we have a baby? Paul had planned to take a sabbatical in Canada after a conference in London and our lives were on a harmonious, even keel. The two of us talked as we walked and, for the first time, we finally agreed.

A few days later we went to Pretoria for Thabo Mbeki's inauguration as president. I packed a sari and a short-sleeved blouse and sandals, only to arrive in a rainy, windy city. The room we were booked into had faulty heating, and in the freezing cold Paul and I kept each other warm in time-honoured fashion. We

woke early the next morning for the long, tedious, miserably cold trip to the inauguration. Not long after, Paul left for London, where I called him the day after his conference had finished. 'Do you remember that decision we took?' I asked. 'Well, that baby must have just been waiting. I think I'm pregnant.'

At the national consultative conference against the sexual exploitation of children held in parliament in early 1999, I had posed the question whether it was possible to use power in new, creative ways. I recalled the vision we'd had when we entered parliament in 1994, of using power 'not to exploit, oppress, cause wars, divide or destroy, but to build and create'. Now I focused on the children and youth: how could we enable them to flower? I quoted my favourite of Khalil Gibran's poems: 'Your children are not your children … They are the sons and daughters of life's longing for itself.' Life longing for itself … Sure enough, during the second election campaign I was pregnant with my third child.

After the elections we returned to the new parliament under President Mbeki. Succeeding Mandela was a tough job for anyone. The transition from Mandela to Mbeki had been filled with speculation and conflict. It was rumoured that Mandela wanted Cyril Ramaphosa as president after him. In the aftermath of the succession battle, Ramaphosa went into business, although he remained on the ANC's national executive committee. He consistently topped the ANC elections at its national conference but chose to remain outside formal politics. Mbeki became deputy president. Five years later he became president and inherited a democracy plagued by the militarised, violent and poverty-ridden legacy of apartheid, which globalisation had compounded. But the 'people of the rainbow' were expected to continue being the 'miracle nation'. Mbeki was not a man for the quick sound-bite and the media characterised him as someone who lacked the

'human touch', constantly contrasting him with his predecessor. Yet he was widely acknowledged as having effectively run the government for Mandela.

In our second parliament, the parliamentary and party hierarchy reconvened committees, enabling them to begin their work. The election rhetoric of commitment to women's rights had faded by the time that the committee on women was reconvened. On the ANC's list of candidates for the second parliament I was the seventeenth woman among hundreds, yet this did not translate into much for the committee which I had chaired. It was the last to be reconvened in October 1999.

At our first meeting I was re-elected as chair by members from across the political parties and we immediately began our work. We considered the controversy surrounding a judgment of Justice John Foxcroft in the Cape High Court. The judge had sentenced a man found guilty of raping his minor daughter to seven years in prison instead of the mandatory life sentence that our first parliament had legislated for those found guilty of raping children. He motivated his ruling by referring to a previous case in which he had been one of the judges. In that case, the presiding judge said of a father who had raped his two young daughters over a period of seven years that 'the father's sexual deviancy was limited to his own family and there was no suggestion that the man's behaviour would surface outside the family unit'. In both cases, the judges adopted the view that rape within the family merited a lesser penalty than rape outside it.

Foxcroft's ruling reasserted the division of the private from the public, the domestic arena from 'society', as if family units were not part of society. We had fought to challenge this division through policy, legislation and budgets. This is the division that silences and makes invisible the terror experienced by children and women who are violated in homes, communities, organisations, religions and countries – terror legitimised by loyalty and patriotism defined by and for the powerful.

In the committee meeting, many of us expressed outrage. We decided to hold hearings and invited stakeholders with power to address the violence in our society that manifests in the brutality of rape, witch-burning, battery, femicide, adult incest with children as well as the everyday humiliation of sexual harassment. The committee agreed that the hearings should highlight the impediments to effective implementation of the laws on violence against women (such as the Domestic Violence Act, the new bail law and the minimum sentences law). The hearings would also examine how these impediments could be removed so that women might enjoy the rights they had won in the new democracy. We were 'committed to ensuring that the laws we pass are not reduced to paper laws with no meaning for improving the lives of women and female children in our country'.

The next day the *Cape Times* headlined its front-page report with 'Foxcroft to be grilled by MPs'. The story below, completely false, read: 'In an unprecedented move a judge is to be summoned to parliament.' By that afternoon, several judges reacted to the report, slamming the committee and me as chair. Fortunately, some were more judicious in their response. The country's two senior judges, Arthur Chaskalson and Ismail Mahomed, were reported in the *Cape Argus* as saying that 'they doubted if parliament had, indeed, called Judge Foxcroft to account'. On that same afternoon I addressed a press conference together with Frene Ginwala, the Speaker of parliament. I knew I had expressed myself strongly on Foxcroft's ruling but was clear I had not asked for him or any other judge to be summoned before the committee. At the press conference I tried to clarify the committee's primary objective in holding the hearings.

But the damage was done and comment damning the committee snowballed, accusing it of wanting to extend the power of the legislature over the judiciary. After that, it was difficult to get the hearings back on track. Eventually only one judge participated, Kate

O'Regan of the Constitutional Court. Her depth of experience and insight enriched the hearings and the final committee report.

With a very limited budget, the committee had to counteract the widespread negative publicity, to return the focus to the real crisis of gender-based violence. I did an interview with Bush Radio, which was copied and sent to community radio stations across the country. In parliament we called for two debates, the first on the challenges facing South Africa in building a non-sexist society, and the second on rape and other forms of violence against women.

In the second debate, unlike the first, I didn't talk about laws, budgets, programmes and institutions. Instead I decided to speak from my heart, trusting that my words would help us go beyond party-political divisions and focus us on the urgency of ending violence. Violence wasn't confined to our country: it was a global phenomenon. But because women in South Africa now refused to be silent, we had a unique opportunity to address the violence that stretched back 'not just to our apartheid, patriarchal and capitalist past, but beyond colonialism, beyond even the biblical era, to deep beliefs about women and men that deny our wholeness ... that set up God as the voice of the Patriarch, rather than God as the voice of unconditional love, who reflects back to us the best of who we can be, both men and women.'

That weekend the *Sunday Independent* outlined the furore around the hearings before reaching a more cheering conclusion:

> Govender has been a driving force in putting women on the agenda in areas previously thought not to be involved with 'women's issues'. When she came to parliament, she took these kinds of issues into committees that weren't expecting them. People in parliament say the result has been dramatic and that departments' budgets are now routinely scrutinised for the way in which women will benefit. Govender has

survived Harold Wilson's 24 hours, with her charm and determination intact. 'We could say our job is done when the law is written,' she said, 'but it isn't. It's only done when we see the laws function and when they're effective. Writing laws is hard, but implementation is harder.'

The headline read: 'Pregs Govender: riding out the storm.' The journalist couldn't have realised how accurately he had captured my life at the time. The request to eliminate an insubordinate woman felt like a tidal wave that threatened to smash everything. Riding through it demanded all the resources I could harness. The energy unleashed within me a steadfast determination to use my power to stand against the elimination of those who were most powerless, most voiceless. It was time to say no.

PART 5

The arms deal

Nineteen

PRIORITIES

The first time we heard about the arms deal was in 1994, when the old South African Defence Force generals, supported by some of our own comrades like Joe Modise, the minister of defence, asked parliament to approve the allocation for it in the Budget. In that debate, full of optimism that we would be true to our promise of 'a better life for all', I argued for cutting military expenditure by 15 per cent and reallocating it to socioeconomic spending. The apartheid government had diverted massive amounts of money into a war against its own citizens; it created a highly militarised state in which women's vaginas and breasts were targeted in particularly vicious ways. In detention rats were pushed into women's vaginas and women's breasts were smashed. In vigilante attacks, pregnant women were disembowelled. Such cruelty against women and girls was perpetuated by strangers as well as loved ones. Despite the cessation of military war and the dismantling of the apartheid state, this silent war continued.

Yet the committee on women was expected to stick to 'women's issues', as if prioritising weapons of war above fully implementing

the Domestic Violence Act did not legitimise the war in bedrooms and borders.

As the debate on defence spending intensified, I was dismissed as lacking the knowledge and experience to make a judgement call on the arms deal and was labelled a pacifist and Gandhian, neither of which I considered myself to be. I was relieved that there were other voices, of those steeped in years of experience in the ANC's defence and intelligence structures, who expressed the same sentiments. Joe Slovo, who used to head Umkhonto weSizwe and was now minister of housing, argued against the arms deal in the same debate.

> I join those who have problems with the overall size of the defence budget; particularly with the appropriations for spending on military hardware and new systems ... We have not been presented in this house or indeed, at any other level of government with a thorough analysis of the potential threats to the security and integrity of South Africa which is capable of convincing me of the need for major capital spending on items such as submarines and ocean-going warships at a time when we face a housing backlog in this country in excess of one million units.

Similar views were taken by the minister of intelligence, Joe Nhlanhla, who in the strategic review had said: 'We all have seen the folly of regarding security in primarily militaristic terms ... Questions raised by ANC MPs on the need to cut spending in these areas, and redirect it to dealing with the pressing social needs and employment creation, are in line with our mandate.' Who should have known better about military spending and the arms deal than the person who used to head the ANC's armed forces and the person who was South Africa's minister of intelligence? In a Budget debate in which I quoted Nhlanhla, I concluded my

speech with a poem by Rabindranath Tagore that used to be a childhood favourite in our home:

> Where the mind is without fear and the head is held high;
> Where knowledge is free;
> Where the world has not been broken into fragments by narrow domestic walls;
> Where the clear stream of reason has not lost its way into the dreary desert sand of dead habit …,
> into that place of freedom, let my country awake …

For too many, reason had already lost its way as the habits of the old generals became our new standard.

In the early years, there was a spirit of common purpose among women in cabinet, parliament and civil society to tackle the real issues of the country. Spending on arms was not one of them. This strength and resolve was highlighted at the government's conference on its 1996 post-Beijing cabinet commitments. Several women of vision made their mark on the outcome. Prominent among these was Nkosazana Dlamini-Zuma, the minister of health, who had led South Africa's delegation to the United Nations Conference in Beijing. In our first parliamentary term Nkosazana courageously introduced laws against smoking and to ensure affordable medicines, despite well-funded lobbying by the tobacco and pharmaceutical industries.

When it was my turn to speak on the Women's Budget, I argued that a long-term view was essential to breaking the cycles of poverty. I concluded my speech by applying this analysis to the arms deal. 'We must ask departments to put their money where their mouths are – to take away spending in defence on corvettes which cost R434 million each, submarines which cost R1.1 billion each and generals who cost R464 638 each per year.' (By 1999,

government estimated spending over R1.7 billion for each of the three submarines, over R1.7 billion for each of the four corvettes, over R1.9 billion for the Gripen fighter planes and over R7 billion for other aircraft. Current estimates, excluding operational costs, have risen way beyond the figures I used in 1996.)

At the 1996 conference, government announced its most significant post-Beijing cabinet commitment: 'to decrease military expenditure and reallocate the savings to women's empowerment'. It was an incredible commitment but unfortunately didn't last long. By 1998 government had begun negotiating the arms deal, which signalled a return to increased military expenditure. Women's empowerment was no longer a priority for which government was prepared to decrease military spending.

Twenty

VOTING AGAINST
THE ARMS DEAL

In the National Assembly in 2001 we were coming up to the vote on the defence budget. This budget included the arms deal, which was going to cost South Africa billions. I thought of how apartheid had spent huge amounts of South Africa's money waging its terrible war against its citizens. What had happened between 1994 and 2001? It was only seven years since the downfall of apartheid, and we seemed to have forgotten our own priorities. When did we stop listening to ourselves and adopt the position of apartheid's generals?

Redressing apartheid's legacy of poverty and violence as well as the impact of HIV/Aids were critical needs that desperately needed funding. Instead it was the 2001 defence budget vote which was increased, to provide for payments for the arms deal. Even within the defence department there were many other priorities. The racist mind-set that had normalised state-sponsored violence had to be transformed; we had to teach male soldiers to respect women and girls instead of seeing them as objects they could rape at will; soldiers taught to kill had to learn how to create a peaceful society;

retrenched soldiers had be equipped with the skills to ensure that they wouldn't be discarded into unemployment and poverty. Instead of tackling these vital issues we were borrowing money from countries like Britain, Germany and Sweden to buy arms that they themselves found redundant.

And what was the interest on the loans going to cost South Africa? In the ANC caucus, we had been addressed by Alec Erwin, minister of trade and industry. An economist, his work as a Cosatu unionist had been useful to me in preparing union education programmes in the 1980s. Now Alec took care in choosing what to say about allegations that had surfaced in the media of corruption involving one of the arms suppliers and the head of procurement in the defence department, Chippy Shaik. But he admitted, 'What we don't know is how many rands we pay for that Gripen [fighter plane] each year. We do not know what we'll finally pay for this deal.' (Since his presentation to caucus the estimated R29 billion that government projected for the arms deal has more than doubled, excluding hidden costs. Some estimate that it has cost over R100 billion.)

Those who defended the deal maintained that parliament's adoption of the defence review had given government the go-ahead to buy this equipment. I checked this with Laurie Nathan, one of the drafters of the defence White Paper and the defence review. He strongly disputed this interpretation. According to Laurie, parliament's approval of the review was not a mandate to buy weapons. The 'force design', the detailed list of weaponry, was – as the review described it – only a 'vision'. The review clearly stated that the final details 'would inevitably deviate from the vision' and 'such deviations will be subject to parliamentary oversight'. The final list did not come back to parliament's National Assembly or National Council of Provinces, for our approval, before the negotiations for the arms deal began at the end of 1998.

In the caucus, Alec argued that the deal 'would not set back

RDP objectives'. At that point I asked him how we as committees could check whether the spending on the arms deal was in line with ANC priorities and the mandate of government. There were other questions, some of which Barbara Hogan later described as *gatkruiping* (the English term 'brown-nosing' does not quite capture the vividness of the Afrikaans). Alec answered every question except mine – it would need 'a more detailed discussion'. He did not say when or where this would happen and at the time there was no chance to clarify this with him.

After Alec had finished, President Mbeki addressed us in his characteristically quiet, measured tones. My ears pricked up when I heard the words 'I'd like to tell Comrade Pregs'. My heart began thumping and fear closed in before I began to breathe again, began to remember the peace and love of my meditations as he repeated the phrase in his address. He said that we were elected by the ANC. We gained and lost our positions as chairs of committees through the ANC. Chairpersons like me were being given a clear message. Andrew Feinstein, who chaired the ANC study group on public accounts, would be fired from his position in the course of challenging the corruption in the arms deal.

As Mbeki's voice droned on, I slowly made my way back to a quiet place in my heart. I remembered that the ANC was not just the party hierarchy; the ANC was also the poor and the powerless who had voted us into power, who might not even afford membership cards. Their interests could not be ignored in favour of those who made large donations to the party. I meditated on the power of love and, despite my initial trepidation, began to feel a calm power fill me. When Mbeki delivered his famous 'I am an African' poem-speech to parliament years earlier, this power had shone in his obvious self-respect and respect for us all. In his talks on the arms deal and on HIV/Aids, I listened and longed to hear this power resonate in our president's voice once again.

Within the ANC several of us worked hard on a range of matters about the arms deal. The ANC study group on public accounts, with Andrew as chair, scrutinised the arms deal and exposed the devil in the detail. Andrew refused to bow to the resulting political pressure and continued to raise uncomfortable questions – the answers to which are now emerging quite dramatically. Barbara Hogan, who had been imprisoned for ten years by the apartheid state, provided important political support to Andrew during this time. The study group was up against powerful people like Chippy Shaik, head of procurement policy in the defence ministry. He had allegedly abused his position to secure contracts for his brother Schabir, who was also financial adviser to Deputy President Jacob Zuma. Out of the blue Gavin Woods, from the IFP, who chaired the public accounts committee, received a letter signed by Zuma, demanding that the committee stop their investigations. Woods eventually resigned as chair. Andrew, who had a young child, experienced a burglary at his home, in which only files related to the arms deal were stolen. Apart from Woods, another opposition party MP, Patricia de Lille, then in the PAC, played an important role in publicly exposing details of the corruption (her source of information allegedly being an ANC intelligence cadre).

My own challenge to the arms deal from 1994 was that it was an entirely misplaced priority. I also assumed that corruption would inevitably follow the arms deal, as it had in most countries. It is common knowledge that the international dealers in arms build in the costs of bribery and corruption in deals like this. The countries that sell us arms have a lot to answer for but it is unlikely that they will be called to account. Where someone is corrupted, someone is doing the corrupting, and both are equally liable.

Our country's money was needed to end the relentless poverty and reconstruct our society. I interrogated ministers who came before the committee on women as to why funds were not available

for basic things like land, housing, water and job creation or to address gender-based violence and HIV/Aids, yet billions were being spent on arms. Several ministers responded by referring to the 'offsets', the promise made by the arms companies to create jobs in exchange for securing the contracts. I began to analyse what the offsets meant. Ministers insisted that the 'offsets' were worth an estimated R110 billion and would generate 64 000 new jobs. I learnt that offsets are actually standard promises made by arms dealers to clinch deals, and never materialise to any substantial degree. Even the suppliers scorned them. Roger Hallhag, adviser to the Swedish prime minister, commented that because offsets are so open to corruption they are internationally discredited, and even forbidden in some countries – though he added patronisingly, 'Lower standards apply in third-world countries.' Topping that, the South African magazine *Noseweek* quoted a senior executive of Saab (the Swedish manufacturer of the Gripens, which Sweden itself no longer used), who said about the South African negotiators in the arms deal, 'There is a great intellectual problem. Those who decide cannot follow in the maze of figures.'

In researching the global arms industry, my impression of its immense power was confirmed. It deliberately foments war and conflict across the world and reaps enormous profit, as exposés of the US and UK war against Iraq prove. My Swedish friend Magnus Walan, a committed anti-apartheid activist, was furious with his government over the arms deal with South Africa. 'It is disgraceful! Our government knows that South Africa needs to spend its money on poverty. It knows this better than most governments. Yet they are only interested in making money out of South Africa, through this arms deal. It is wrong, wrong, wrong!' Magnus sent me information from Sweden as well as internet links to international research organisations critical of the arms industry.

Alec Erwin told caucus that the economist Stephen Gelb had compiled an affordability report for the Treasury, but he did not

divulge the conclusions. I received extracts from the leaked report, which revealed that Gelb's report had warned that the risks of the arms deal were immense and that as a result the government could be faced with 'mounting economic, fiscal and financial difficulties'.

The day before the vote on the defence budget in 2001, I travelled to Johannesburg. On the flight I used the time to collect my thoughts and write down the points I wanted to raise when I reached Luthuli House, ANC headquarters. Albert Luthuli, president of the ANC, and the first South African to win the Nobel Peace Prize, had once argued:

> What must we do to meet this challenge of being spiritually if not physically destroyed as a people? Develop in you the spirit of resisting anything that curbs or limits the development of your talents to their fullest capacity [and] cultivate a sense of service and sacrifice without which Africans can never gain freedom. Freedom comes only to people who are prepared to pay dearly for it.

I was visiting Luthuli House to meet with the secretary-general of the ANC, Kgalema Motlanthe, and the assistant secretary-general, Thenjiwe Mtintso. Paul had worked with Kgalema, then general secretary of the National Union of Mineworkers, when he had been their lawyer, and had been impressed by Kgalema's dedication to workers. Thenjiwe, a feminist communist, had been a leader in the ANC's armed wing and chair of South Africa's first gender commission. In the ANC camps she had taken a stand against the chauvinism of those who made women soldiers clean up after them, reducing courageous women to personal servants and concubines. As a parliamentarian in the defence committee she had forcefully

argued for decreasing military expenditure. Now, in our meeting, Thenjiwe, still engaged in the struggle for equality, looked ill.

I had come to explain what I planned to do about the arms deal, and felt the nerves gnawing in my stomach. There was a dignity in their bearing as they welcomed me to sit with them around the small table in Kgalema's office. I began with the point that the ANC had rejected the arms deal when the old apartheid generals brought it to parliament in 1994. 'Everyone then seemed to be clear that our priority had to be socioeconomic reconstruction,' I said. 'In fact, Thenji, you opposed the deal from 1994 and argued your position in parliament. What made us change our policy?'

Kgalema and Thenjiwe did not pretend to understand the rationale behind the decision. I asked where the decision had been made as it was not discussed and agreed in our parliamentary caucus.

'Was it discussed and agreed in the NEC [the National Executive Committee]?'

Kgalema was thoughtful and clear. 'You are right to ask that question. It was not discussed and agreed to at the NEC.'

'But the NEC is the highest decision-making body of the ANC. If the decision was not made there, who made it and on what basis?'

Kgalema shook his head. 'I'm afraid, Comrade Pregs, that there are too many crucial decisions that are being made outside the NEC.'

I told them I'd decided to vote against the arms deal. Then I was going to resign from parliament as soon as I had wrapped up my work and made a recommendation as to who could replace me as chair of the women's committee – it would take about six more months. I had thoroughly enjoyed my work as an MP since 1994, despite the difficulties. But with the arms deal I had begun to feel worn down by the way cabinet seemed to ignore the needs of the majority of people who had voted us into power. I had grappled with the question of who ANC MPs, including

myself, should be loyal to. There were new values and priorities underlying policy choices such as the arms deal, and parliament's power to influence the course we were now on was severely limited. Though Kgalema and Thenji respectfully accepted my decision to oppose the arms deal, they were shocked at my decision to resign and tried to persuade me to carry on with my work in parliament, particularly in the area of women's rights. But my mind was made up.

In the National Assembly we stood for parliament's customary moment of silence before the vote on the defence budget. I tried to centre myself to act with clarity. I had already decided that I would register my opposition to the arms deal, yet I still felt an anxiety that made me scribble a note to Andrew: 'What are you going to do?' As someone who had already been axed from his position as chair of the ANC study group and would later resign in protest, I knew he would understand my anxiety. I knew I could not walk out of the chamber, away from this vote, as MPs sometimes did, nor could I sit without registering anything. The vote held a powerful message. We had been voted into power by millions who were still waiting patiently for the changes they were promised; they trusted that once in government we would not trash their hopes and dreams. In the National Assembly, breathing into the fear that was rumbling through me, I pressed the yellow button, registering my opposition to the arms deal.

It was a matter of minutes before a tall young Afrikaner ANC MP, Andries Nel, who is today acting chief whip, walked over to me. 'Comrade Pregs, the chief whip has asked me to come to check something with you. It seems that there may have been a problem with the computers.'

'No, Comrade, the computers are correct. They accurately reflect my vote.'

He was red, flustered by my response. I felt sorry for him. He would have to explain this to Tony Yengeni, the chief whip. I tried to help. 'I saw the secretary-general and the deputy secretary-general yesterday in Johannesburg. I told them what I was going to do.' He cut me short – he did not want to hear any more than he had been instructed to; perhaps it would have compromised him. He hurried back to report to Yengeni as a quiet calm descended on me.

Twenty-one

CONSEQUENCES

Shortly after voting against the arms deal, I took part in the national gender summit convened by the Commission for Gender Equality. The minister in charge of the office on the status of women, Essop Pahad, and I sat next to each other, as we were on the same panel.

Before I began my speech I asked all the participants to close their eyes and focus on the power of love and courage within their hearts. I heard the minister breathe out his exasperation. At the end of the short exercise, I asked participants to hold the hand of the person next to them and consciously send that power to them, so that 'we may work with this power rather than the power of hate and fear that drove apartheid, slavery, Nazism and all the other wars that have plagued humanity'. As I reached out my hand to the minister at my side, he clicked his tongue angrily.

The summit seemed to me a good moment to remind the women's movement of the immense challenge we had faced in 1994 and which we continue to face in South African society:

how to ensure that women gained political power rather than dependence on patronage and goodwill. We needed to have the courage to use our power in the interests of all women, particularly the poorest, advancing their cause even when insulted, dismissed, or rendered invisible and marginal.

In the early 1990s the women's movement had not been prepared for becoming part of a global economy based on profit which had deepened the gaping divide between rich and poor. Globally, violence against women and the poor had increased, along with fundamentalism and militarisation. In my view the extent to which our new democracy conformed to or confronted these global trends would have major implications for the feminist agenda of changing the lives of women, especially the poorest, and transforming gendered roles and relationships. As I argued before the summit, one of the ways in which this agenda could be advanced was by ensuring that all legislation that went before cabinet, including the national Budget, had to include an explanation of how it integrated a gender perspective in its formulation.

When the minister spoke, he began with a pointed reference to the fact that he knew the chair of the gender commission, Joyce Seroke, 'from the 1950s, from years back', and went on: 'Joyce and other stalwarts are unlike those Johnny-come-latelies who suddenly come from nowhere, with no experience with poor African women and talk on their behalf.' Apart from attacking me, he was implying that it was only African women who should speak about these issues, while, blind to the irony, he, an Indian man, claimed his right to talk on behalf of all of us.

His speech worked up into a minor frenzy. 'And this thing that Pregs did not vote for the arms deal – if that is so, well, we will deal with her in other forums. But she is talking absolute nonsense about women and poverty. Absolute nonsense!' Before he could proceed any further, Pahad was cut short by booing. He

was clearly taken aback and tried to change tack. A small but significant number of delegates, all African women, stood up to challenge what he had said about poverty. Ayanda Mvimbi, a tall, striking young woman from the Gender Advocacy Project, was one of the first to take the mike. She dared the minister to dispute the fact that African women in South Africa were getting poorer.

That Friday the *Mail & Guardian* reported: 'This week angry delegates said they were "horrified" at how Minister in the Office of the President Essop Pahad "harangued" women at the summit. But he did not succeed with the intimidation, they said. Pahad received a tongue-lashing for the government's arms spending instead of improving the lives of women and eradicating poverty.' The *Sunday Independent* carried an article headlined: 'Minister booed over denial of women's needs.' The reporter revealed that I was 'the only ANC MP who did not vote for the defence budget when it came before parliament at the end of the last parliamentary session.' It was clearly not only the chief whip who had scrutinised the voting record.

Criticism from the minister was not unexpected and it did not push me off course. I found it much harder dealing with criticism from women comrades. One incident that shook me badly took place in Durban in August 2001. It was during the International World Court of Women against Racism, which heard testimonies from women from across the globe, on all wars, including the wars of poverty, genocide and racism. I had been asked to testify as an expert witness on 'exterminating the other'. The apartheid state, like the global arms industry, was expert at 'exterminating the other', so all of us who had fought against apartheid as well as those who opposed the arms industry were in a sense 'expert witnesses'. As I prepared my speech in my

commissar's and my old home-town, the words 'eliminate' and 'exterminate' rhymed in my head like the poetry my daughter Parusha was creating at the time.

As I stood behind the stage, an old friend and comrade, who was now a senior member of government, came up to me. In the course of our discussion I shared with her my decision to vote against the arms deal, which I thought she was already aware of. I was confident that she would agree with how I voted and with my conviction that the money for the arms deal should be used to redress poverty, HIV/Aids and violence. I assumed she would support my action as an act of loyalty to women who had voted for the ANC. But instead she was furious. 'How dare you stab the organisation which nurtured you all these years? How dare you betray our organisation?' she shouted. At that point she was not prepared to challenge the leadership of our organisation on issues I was sure she herself knew were wrong. But I was still shaken by her hostility.

My work and friendships with women reflect my strengths and weaknesses. I had not grown up with sisters and, although I love my brothers dearly, I always yearned for what I imagined other sisters shared. Ignorant, I idealised the relationship and was often ill prepared to deal with harsh words or actions. My comrade and I had reached a painful point in our friendship. For me, this was much harder than attacks from the minister in charge of women. I could deal with the minister's rudeness because his words were those of a relative stranger whose only power was the power to strip away status and privilege. In contrast, I found it hard to accept being erased by those I loved. The angry words of my friend charted a direct course into my heart.

When I took the podium at the court I had to breathe deeply to stop the tears which threatened to disrupt the calm I needed. I began my address with a poem I had written while

trying to understand what had happened to beloved friends and comrades. It was a poem that I would quote again and again over the next year:

we live and speak
no longer conscious
of our wholeness
our connectedness

we have begun to believe
we are fragments
our stories
disconnected
from each other's

we no longer hear our own voices
we no longer see our own faces ...

PART 6

No HIV/Aids

Twenty-two

PATENT RIGHTS
AND HIV/AIDS

It was only in parliament's second term that I began to play any part in tackling the question of HIV/Aids. Up to then it was more than I could manage, too huge an issue on top of poverty and violence against women, the two other areas on which the committee on women had focused its attention. Now and then my conscience gnawed at me but I comforted myself with the thought that others were doing something about the pandemic.

Yet, the fact is that the gender inequality that is at the heart of the spread of HIV/Aids is also the reason why women and girls experience the worst impact of poverty and violence. Sooner or later the committee on women would have to confront this fact. Yet when I was asked by an NGO, in early 1999, to get involved in a committee on HIV/Aids, I sidestepped the challenge, arguing that others more competent than me, like the chairperson of the health committee, were already involved. But by mid-year, I knew I could no longer absolve myself or the committee from our collective responsibility to learn about the issues and represent the interests of women living with HIV/Aids.

Things had shifted from 1994 when cabinet adopted the first national Aids plan. Even in 1998, Thabo Mbeki, then deputy president, had responded with urgency to the pandemic and called for clarity and compassion. 'HIV/Aids is among us. It is real. HIV/ Aids is not someone else's problem. It is my problem. It is your problem.' At the time of his call I felt confident that government leaders were taking the right steps. South Africa was then leading the fight to ensure that the imperatives of public health superseded commercial interests. The minister of health, Nkosazana Dlamini-Zuma, and her director-general, Olive Shisana, for instance, played a major role in the World Health Organisation (WHO) as Southern African countries joined with others to stop the 'developed' world from blocking our access to affordable and safe generic anti-retroviral (ARV) medicine. As a result the WHO had to adopt a new strategy to monitor the pharmaceutical and public health implications of trade agreements, and consider things like access to and prices of medicines.

At the same time the Treatment Action Campaign (TAC), a formidable organisation, consisting mainly of women, was playing a significant role in the local and international campaign against the greed of the pharmaceutical companies. Such greed motivated the complaint by the United States against Brazil, at the World Trade Organisation, for Brazil's insistence on putting patient rights before the patent rights of pharmaceutical firms. In a public stand, TAC's founder, Zackie Achmat, an ANC member who had contracted HIV, pledged not to treat himself with drugs, which were available to middle-class and rich South Africans through the private sector, until there was free treatment for poor South Africans through the public health system. Access to generic equivalents would enable the state to provide affordable treatment for those who were poor and HIV-positive.

In early 1999 Mbeki defended South Africa's Medicines Act, maintaining government's commitment to affordable medicine

in bilateral trade talks with the United States, in which Al Gore punted the interests of the US pharmaceutical industry. But Mbeki's commitment was dramatically challenged by 39 pharmaceutical companies who sued the president and health minister Zuma for our Medicines Act. They were supported by President Clinton, who also ensured that South Africa was put onto a trade watch-list. It was madness: the president of the richest country in the world was trying to prevent South Africa from providing affordable medicine to its poorest citizens. Despite such powerful opposition, our government, together with the TAC, secured a moral victory when the pharmaceutical companies withdrew their case. This victory could have laid the basis for government to challenge the international patents regime further so as to secure affordable medicine on the scale that was needed. Yet opposing objectives in relation to patents existed within government policy and was reflected in the approach of two key departments. While the department of health argued for greater flexibility around patents, the position of the department of trade and industry prevailed. The result was that South Africa protected patents 'as rigidly as the developed world', to use the words of Edwin Cameron, a gay Appeal Court judge living with Aids. It would not do to take on the power of international capitalism, even though some legal experts argued that there was a clear basis for doing so.

By late 1999 things changed for the worse. In the ANC caucus the Treatment Action Campaign was crudely and falsely labelled an agent of the pharmaceutical industry. President Mbeki also appointed a new health minister, Manto Tshabalala-Msimang, whom I had previously worked with on women's legislative priorities. I had developed great respect for her then. But now she seemed to ignore the clarity she had once articulated in her report on HIV/Aids as chair of parliament's health committee. In parliament, she declared that government would not supply the anti-retroviral drug AZT 'to people infected with HIV/Aids, and

people who have been infected through rape or needle-pricks on two grounds: affordability and ... the absence of proper research on the possible side-effects of AZT, in particular its toxic profile'.

Heavily pregnant, I sat listening to her, after hours of chairing hearings on violence against women and access to justice. As a medical doctor herself, the minister must have known that all serious medications have side-effects that have to be clinically managed. To crown it all, we had the ludicrous situation of the minister distributing copies of a chapter from a book by the Aids dissident William Cooper, who claimed that the 'Illuminati' (a group of Jews, communists and international bankers) had introduced Aids to Africa to reduce its population. But HIV/Aids was not ludicrous. As chair of the committee on women, I had position and power. I could no longer sit back and watch from the sidelines as huge numbers of people, most of whom were women, most of whom were poor, were being eliminated not just by HIV/ Aids but by a denial of the reality of the disease.

Twenty-three

OUR CHILDREN

In early 2000 my third baby began his journey into the world. My water bag broke at about midnight. As I went into labour for him I felt calm, clear that his birth would be completely natural. It was five days before I turned 40, but I had practised yoga through most of my pregnancy and felt confident that the birth would be uncomplicated. However, he took his time coming out. In the ward, as Paul and I waited, I practised my yoga. In the early morning we walked around the hospital grounds till the sun got too fierce. I submerged myself in the hospital's hot bath, which was designed to relax the birth muscles. The aromatherapy oil smelt wonderful but did not have the effect I needed. Only late in the afternoon did the contractions heighten. My good intention to have a completely natural birth rapidly vanished after a particularly painful contraction. I dug into Paul's arm and yelled to my gynaecologist through clenched teeth, 'Joy, get me the drug – now, now!'

She swung into action. The epidural worked quickly. Soon I was sitting up laughing, holding the beautiful carved mirror Parusha

gave me and in it I watched our baby emerge. Paul, looking slightly shell-shocked, could not take his eyes off his first baby, and for the next few nights slept on a chair next to us. When the nurses demanded our baby – they needed to take him away to be washed and weighed – I insisted they bring the scale and bath to me. He was on my breast when Parusha and Yashodan arrived and bonded with their little baby brother. They stayed while he was washed and took turns holding him on their chests.

Meanwhile, at home the renovations which should have been completed were still proceeding. I remained in hospital for a week, hoping that the builders would be finished by then, but they were still there when we got home. A few weeks later I lost my temper and demanded that they get done, clear up, and clear out, immediately! The dust disappeared as they miraculously wrapped up the work and restored our home to us. Clearly, there is nothing like the contained, well-directed rage of a new mother.

Our baby was a few weeks old when we invited our large extended family over for his naming ceremony. Naming a child is not easy. We received a wide range of suggestions. Paul had the final say as I had chosen both Parusha's and Yashodan's names. He eventually chose Saien, which is Tamil for 'blessing' as well as 'blessed'. All Saien's family took turns gently rocking him in my wedding sari. We planted trees for him in the garden, and in the following months they began to take root; today they stand taller than Saien, who is now seven years old. Today the trees flower alongside the gigantic mealies, lush spinach and the sweetest peas that Saien planted himself. Saien's love for gardening vegetables and his determined insistence on thinking for himself inspired me to follow his example when he stopped eating meat a year ago.

But in the year of Saien's birth, many other children were bearing the brunt of a terrible disregard that was growing at the highest

levels of power in the country as the ancient principle of *ubuntu* – signifying the deepest respect for others – was discarded in favour of expedience.

The choices I had over my health and during childbirth were still not available to most women. In fact, the choices for poor women who were HIV-positive, contrary to all that we had fought for, were being diminished, not just by the illness, but by the state's response. At that time Parks Mankahlana, the spokesperson for President Mbeki, was interviewed by *Science* magazine about why the department of health refused to provide ARV medicine to pregnant women. 'That mother is going to die and that HIV-negative child will be an orphan. That child must be brought up. Who is going to bring that child up? It's the state, the state. That's resources, you see.' The simple logic that we should use treatment to save the babies as well as the mothers escaped Parks and some international donors who sponsor treatment programmes for babies but will not pay for treatment for mothers. Neither the state nor Parks seemed prepared to acknowledge their responsibility for the children. Like other comrades, in his private life Parks refused to pay maintenance for two of his children until ordered to do so by the courts.

Parks also announced that President Mbeki had convened an international panel of experts to resolve 'whether there is this thing called Aids, what it is, whether HIV leads to Aids, whether there is something called HIV'. The panel met and their deliberations began, issuing in a controversial report that did not help the situation on the ground at all. How could we move forward when the presidential Aids advisory panel was still debating, even if in more sophisticated terms than those Parks used, whether there was 'a thing called Aids'? Both in parliament and in the ANC caucus, the reasons for government's refusal to provide ARV medicine shifted from doubting the link between HIV and Aids to toxicity and affordability, and round and round in circles. A fruitless

debate, it had dire repercussions, as ARV treatment is premised on the scientific conclusion that a virus, HIV, causes Aids. Parks himself died a few months later, reportedly from Aids.

Saien was about three months old when parliament appointed me a member of the official South African delegation to the United Nations review of governments' commitments to the platform of action adopted in Beijing five years previously. I agreed to attend and took Saien with me. Paul, who had just returned from working in Geneva, volunteered to look after him while I attended the meetings. I was still breastfeeding Saien and expected to take him into the sessions with me when I needed to. In New York, the security woman said as we stood in the queue to get security clearance, 'I hope yuh don't think yuh are taking him with yuh. Children ain't allowed into the UN General Assembly.' 'He will be coming with me,' I told her firmly, before we sat down for the photos for our security cards. The South African delegation and our UN representative supported me on this issue. In the conference I came across Angela King, the gentle and dignified adviser to UN Secretary General Kofi Annan. We'd met before when she'd headed the UN team monitoring our election in 1994. In her strong Caribbean accent, she informed me that she'd heard I was bringing my baby with me and had made arrangements for a breastfeeding room. The guards may have been following old guidelines, but some women were thinking way ahead of their institutions.

As it turned out, the air-conditioned UN buildings were much too cold for our small baby. Paul and I decided it would be wiser for him to remain in the hotel room, especially at night. As our delegation stayed across the road from the UN buildings, I could easily walk back to breastfeed him. One night at about 2 am, I ran back to the hotel room, breastfed Saien, and was running back to the UN when the absurdity of it all hit me. I was not going to change anything at the meeting that night. There were others

far better qualified than me and far more energised. As I turned back to the hotel I realised I hadn't had a full night's sleep since I arrived and was utterly exhausted.

<p style="text-align:center">◎</p>

Beijing Plus Five was a challenging time for the women's movement. In the preceding years an unholy alliance had been forged between the US government, traditional religious groups including the Catholic Church, and some new fundamentalist Christian and Islamic groups. Women's bodies were once again the battleground with every authoritarian power attempting to assert control. The ancient equation of sex equals sin equals temptation by women had reasserted itself powerfully around HIV/Aids as women were cast as both the cause (as whore) and the cure (as virgin).

At the UN, this negative bloc, opposed to abortion and condoms, and in favour of sexual abstinence and the death penalty, pitted itself against the progressive women's movement. They tried undoing the gains made at the Beijing conference, such as the right to reproductive choice and the right to challenge the adverse impact of globalisation on women. At Beijing Plus Five, however, the global women's movement succeeded in holding back the tide and the final document that came out of the meeting upheld the original position enunciated at Beijing in 1995. An important ideological battle had been won.

It did trouble me, though, that so many feminist activists should be pouring our energy, resources and time into a process dominated by those who had far greater resources to tie up meetings in endless bureaucratic quibbling. Was the energy and focus of the women's movement being diverted away from tackling the actual problems? I decided that there was a need to respect what each of us did best. As I made clear in a speech to the massive Japanese delegation to Beijing Plus Five, women had to use the power we had to benefit

the poorest of women. The policies we fought for 'could not be the policies of division, exclusion or elitism. Unless women draw on each other and support each other, we are going to be co-opted, no matter how large our numbers.' This observation would prove dishearteningly true of the response to HIV/Aids by many South African women in power.

<center>◎</center>

At home one evening in June 2000, while breastfeeding Saien, I watched the coverage on TV of a march in Durban organised by TAC during the international Aids conference. Their poster was painted a vivid red, and contained a child's face imprinted with the words 'One Aids death every 10 minutes'. It was prophetic of the fate of Nkosi Johnson, a passionate Aids activist who addressed the conference and who soon afterwards died at the age of 12. While Nkosi was still speaking, President Mbeki left the conference. His departure at that moment was a sign of the blindness which would later lead him to say he did not know anyone who had died of Aids.

A month later Beryl Lockman, then 28 years old, died of Aids. She was the granddaughter of Walter Sisulu's sister Rosabella. The family had to decide whether to disclose that the cause of death was Aids. Walter himself, whose words, presence and actions embodied the best in the male leadership in the ANC, was an astute and humble man, and his marriage to Albertina was characterised by gentle, romantic caring. They chose their son Max to disclose publicly the true cause of Beryl's death. Max noted that this decision was taken at a family meeting at which everyone was present: a reflection of the family's commitment to fight HIV/Aids.

It was precisely this open and dignified acknowledgement of the reality of Aids that was needed in government's public pronouncements – and was so lacking. Around this time, President

Mbeki addressed us in the ANC caucus on HIV/Aids. There, and later on in both parliament and the media, what he said directly undermined the commitment and conviction of his 1998 speech. As he spoke in the caucus, I made notes and wanted to ask him why we were not challenging the real issue of the power of pharmaceutical firms and of governments like the United States which placed profits from patents above the lives of those with HIV/Aids. Instead Mbeki talked of conspiracy and distracted us into a debate about whether a virus can cause a syndrome. When Mbeki sat down, I put up my hand to raise my questions. Comrades seated nearby glanced sideways at me, their eyes urging me to put my hand down. The chairperson looked away, saying that there was to be no discussion, and moved swiftly on to the next item on the agenda. Clearly, others in caucus were as stunned as I was at the president's comments. One of them must have leaked Mbeki's address to the *Mail & Guardian*, which published an accurate report of what he'd said.

Soon afterwards President Mbeki addressed parliament on HIV/ Aids. I sat hoping that he would talk with the clarity we'd respected before. Instead he only deepened the confusion as he repeated, no longer in the relative privacy of the ANC caucus but in the glare of the world media, 'How can a virus cause a syndrome?'

When I tried to understand what I saw as a growing confusion, a friend in the cabinet said: 'You don't understand the complexity of the issues like we do. It is not as simple as you think. I wish you could hear the information that is presented to us in cabinet.'

'Then help me understand,' I replied. 'Why should people who are poor die from a disease that we would receive treatment for, from our medical aid? We use medicine all the time: I chose the epidural when all the natural options failed to ease the pain. Why can't all women make choices around what is best for our own bodies? What makes this disease different from cancer or any other life-threatening illness? Cancer patients can choose whether

or not to have chemotherapy in public hospitals even though the side-effects are horrible.'

My comrade shook her head. 'This HIV/Aids thing is too complex. Also,' she added decisively, calling for closure, 'we are not allowed to discuss confidential information.'

As I saw it, my intelligent comrade failed to match the 'complex' arguments and information the president provided in cabinet with what she saw with her own eyes. What did it mean to be a loyal party member when mothers, fathers, daughters, sons, brothers and sisters, husbands and wives, were dying of HIV/Aids? Over and over again the same thing was repeated: 'The president is a very intelligent man. He is extremely well read. He does his homework' – until I wanted to scream out, 'Yes, but he's not infallible. He needs to look at what's actually happening. He doesn't need defenders, we're not out to destroy him – we want him to beat HIV/Aids and end economic apartheid everywhere.' In the ANC caucus and in parliament I looked at Thabo Mbeki, son of Govan and Epainette, and wanted him to open his eyes to what was happening to women who have HIV/Aids, and use his power for their lives.

I could no longer stand aside. In October 2000 I decided that it was time that the committee on women developed its own understanding, not just of the problem but of solutions. I asked two of parliament's best researchers, Nazeema Ahmed and Carmine Rustin, to investigate and develop research briefs for the committee on several issues: women and HIV/Aids, generic medicines, multilateral trade agreements, the Brazilian national drug policy, the government's mother-to-child transmission policy and programme, and its policy on the treatment of rape survivors. The research briefs were ready in November and copies were circulated to committee members. We also commissioned Masimanyane, an organisation based in the Eastern Cape, to research the situation of women and HIV/Aids in five provinces. We asked Case to

survey HIV/Aids service organisations to find out what type of programmes and projects existed and in which areas; the funding received; and how government could assist them to provide services to help people, households and communities affected by HIV/Aids. We had to understand what was going on and how the committee could intervene most effectively to improve the lives of women with HIV/Aids. That was our mandate, as our very long committee name spelt out.

Later that year an organisation in Mpumalanga called Grip, the Greater Nelspruit Rape Intervention Project, approached us to say that they had been ordered to stop providing ARV treatment to rape survivors who were under threat of contracting HIV/Aids. Someone in our ANC study group cynically observed, 'They're just a group of conservative white women who don't mind experimenting with our people's lives.' It was true that many conservative groups had latched onto HIV/Aids to punt their own agendas. But Grip's reports clearly showed that it, like many other organisations, seemed to be responding to the crisis of gender-based violence. After being asked to stop providing post-exposure prophylaxis to rape survivors, Grip was evicted from the Rob Ferreira Hospital on the orders of the female provincial minister of health. By this stage they had helped 74 rape survivors, half of whom were under 16 years of age. Grip took the department to the High Court and the department was forced to settle.

The following year I received a letter from Amnesty International saying that in the same province the provincial minister had issued threats of dismissal to doctors providing ARVs to rape survivors. We discussed Amnesty's letter in the committee and delegated Priscilla Themba, our deputy chair, who was from Mpumalanga, to meet with this minister to try to resolve the situation. Though Priscilla met with her, the report-back showed us clearly that there was no possibility of resolution.

At the root of the growing confusion in the state and among

its officials about the implementation of the government's HIV/ Aids policy was the president's questioning of its basic premise: that HIV caused Aids. Instead of challenging this, the health minister added to the confusion. There was a glaring contradiction between Mbeki's position on the arms deal, his stated commitment to ending poverty and his position on HIV/Aids. We all agreed with him that poverty exacerbated Aids. No one could argue with the fact that poverty weakened the immune system, creating an environment in which the virus could thrive. But Mbeki implied that poverty actually *caused* Aids. Many of Mbeki's trusted foot-soldiers such as the health minister and some of the provincial ministers were using their power to refuse to provide treatment for HIV/Aids in public hospitals and clinics, either to prevent transmission of HIV from mother to child or in circumstances such as rape, which exacerbated the possibility of contracting HIV. In this way they contributed to the suffering and early death of those who were HIV-positive, poor and dependent on the public health system – and they were being promoted for doing so.

At the same time, all of us MPs, ministers, MECs, government bureaucrats and the president himself belonged to a medical aid with cover for HIV/Aids, including ARV treatment, which we could draw on if we or our children were raped or contracted HIV/ Aids. We could afford skilled doctors to help manage the side-effects. Our medical aid even covered a host of alternative healing modalities, including traditional medicine. We, who were denying choice to others, had real choices. As I celebrated my baby's first birthday, I could not ignore what was happening to other women and their children.

Twenty-four

STAND UP
FOR OUR LIVES

In 2001 I used my position as committee chair to initiate hearings on HIV/Aids. I wanted women's voices to be heard by President Mbeki. I hoped that if the information was presented to the president, he would act on it. Perhaps he was surrounded by too many sycophants, all afraid to 'speak truth to power'. I believed that the public hearings would bring ministers and ordinary MPs far closer to women with HIV/Aids, and to the scientists, doctors, experts and practitioners who worked daily with the problem. We had to cut through the fear and the authoritarianism we had submitted to when we reneged on the government's own 2000–2005 HIV/Aids plan to ensure treatment as well as prevention.

Our committee announced the holding of public hearings on how South Africa could best address the impact of HIV/Aids on women and girls. Even though we began at the height of the HIV/Aids controversy, I was emboldened by the words of our former president, Nelson Mandela, who was moved to plead at the International Aids Conference:

If 27 years in prison have done anything to us, it is to use the silence of solitude to make us understand how precious words are and how real speech is in its impact upon the way people live and die ... the poor on our continent would, if anyone cared to ask their opinions, wish that the dispute about the primacy of politics or science be put on the backburner and that we proceed to address the needs and concerns of those suffering and dying.

I asked Abe Nkomo, chair of the parliamentary health committee, for a copy of their report on hearings they had held in May 2000. It seemed to have vanished into parliament's bureaucracy and it took a while before a copy was located. Abe's report argued that the South African government needed to use the scope of the Medicines Act and exemptions from TRIPS, the trade-related aspects of the intellectual property rights agreement, to access and eventually produce good-quality generics so that affordable treatment could be available for HIV-positive patients who needed it. The recommendations in Abe's report had not been implemented, and no one had even mentioned them.

Our committee's hearings began in September and ended in October 2001. We heard the testimonies and recommendations of many people, some of whom had experienced the effects of HIV/ Aids at first hand and gave moving addresses. There were many submissions which dealt in detail with the social and economic reasons why women and girls bore the worst brunt of HIV/Aids, These included the powerlessness of poverty; job losses in the formal sector, which pushed women and girls into prostitution; traditional gender roles; definitions of masculinity premised on multiple relationships with no responsibility for contraception; dry 'skin to skin' sex; violent coercion as the first experience of sex for many girls; and the belief that raping a virgin could cure HIV/Aids. Amidst all these problems there were also innovative solutions

such as female-controlled prevention methods; a campaign to mobilise men to educate other men about joint responsibility and respect for the sexual rights of women and girls; and academic research that was not controlled by pharmaceuticals with a narrow profit agenda. However, there remained a major stumbling block to the prospect of South Africans developing a unified national response.

On 23 September the president of the Medical Research Council (MRC), Professor Makgoba, was to address us on the MRC report on HIV/Aids. This report revealed that Aids was the biggest killer in our country. It estimated that 40 per cent of adult deaths in the 15–49 age group in 2000 were due to Aids and that between 5 and 7 million South Africans would die from it by 2010. Shortly before the hearing Professor Makgoba sent a fax apologising that he couldn't attend, due to 'urgent MRC matters'. There was much speculation as to why he suddenly cancelled, especially when, soon afterwards, President Mbeki disputed the MRC's statistics and quoted outdated 1995 WHO figures for Africa showing that heart disease and malaria were the two biggest killers. That weekend, the ANC health committee secretary, Saadiq Kariem, was quoted in the media as saying, 'My opinion is that we need to make sure that our judgements are scientifically based. We've obviously got to use the latest figures.' The committee agreed.

In our hearing with the health department we simply had a bureaucrat re-reading the government's 2000–2005 HIV/Aids plan with which we agreed but which lacked political will, time frames and resources for implementation. Their departmental team included a female director, Dr Kamy Chetty, who listened in silence to his presentation. Kamy, whom I had first met when we were student activists, looked embarrassed. She surely knew the truth about HIV/Aids that her minister seemed to be denying. Their spokesperson was clearly nervous and kept saying he was unable to answer even the simplest questions posed by the committee, as

'only the minister can deal with that'. It was frustrating. 'If you are not empowered to address any questions at all, surely we should hear from the minister herself, who has the power to respond to our questions,' I advised. This was the key department, and they had sent a bureaucrat who had no power.

Shortly after tea the health minister flew in. She wanted to address us immediately. Although the director-general of social development had arrived punctually, she graciously agreed to be rescheduled. Manto Tshabalala-Msimang was furious as she lectured the committee in a rapid-gunfire way, mainly arguing against the MRC report. When she was through, she left without any discussion. Her hostile manner seemed to us to undermine the good work that many people in her department were doing. In fact the health department in the Western Cape, under an ANC member, Dr Faried Abdullah, directed the largest treatment programme in Khayelitsha township, on which he had reported to our hearings.

The departments of education and trade and industry gave submissions on the programmes they had instituted. All these government departments were doing commendable work, but there was no coherent, overall leadership to pull the diverse initiatives together. The lack of political will was already clear to us: not a single minister apart from Tshabalala-Msimang, who arrived unexpectedly and in response to our prompting, had accepted our invitation to address the hearings.

But Dr Olive Shisana, the former director-general of health and head of the HIV/Aids directorate of the Human Sciences Research Council, stepped forward. A formidable scientist, she contradicted Mbeki's insistence that the biggest killers were heart disease and malaria. 'HIV/Aids is the leading cause of death on the African continent,' she asserted. She also challenged the toxicity argument of the president and the health minister as she explained, 'There is not a single medicine that has no side-effect.' Olive explained how

government could provide affordable treatment through importing ARVs and other medicines from countries like Brazil and Thailand and learning from these countries to produce generic medicines. Olive also explained how South Africa's government could use the TRIPS exemptions to make affordable generic medicines on patented drugs available to poor patients.

We received the Brazilian national drug policy together with a paper, 'Brazil: people first, profits later', from their health ministry. Brazil had faced similar predictions to South Africa of a looming HIV/Aids crisis in the early 1990s. In response, it had developed a comprehensive prevention and treatment campaign. Their policy choice to provide free ARV treatment was a powerful incentive for Brazilians to get an Aids test and begin to prevent the spread of HIV. This decision led to a 50 per cent reduction in Brazil's mortality rate. In the document, the head of Brazil's Aids programme explained how prejudiced critics such as senior US government officials had been confounded. 'The main criticism from developed countries was that we did not have the conditions for ARV treatment. They said it would be dangerous for other countries, that we would cause resistance. They also said that uneducated people can't stick to their treatment regime, that it was too expensive, and that our health system was too fragile.' The critics were proved wrong on all counts.

We noted Brazil's efficiency. In 1994, when we voted in our democracy, Brazil's government began producing generic equivalents of ARVs in their state laboratories. By 1996 they had passed intellectual property legislation to enable Brazil to import and produce generic ARVs. The cost-saving from declining hospitalisation and treatment for opportunistic diseases which flourished on Aids-weakened immune systems offset about 85 per cent of the cost of ARVs.

Then came the eye-opener. Brazil had offered to transfer the technology they had developed for making generic ARVs. They

were prepared to train other countries in the practicalities of treatment. The obvious question was why our government had not accepted Brazil's offer. The answer has nothing to do with the debate about whether HIV causes Aids, but is about how the world trade system keeps sovereign states in line. The World Trade Organisation promotes the interests of large companies like the pharmaceuticals against the poor, despite Clinton's seemingly magnanimous exemption. Yet it was our government's choice to challenge or collude with the US and the undemocratic processes of the WTO that are slanted in favour of the rich and the powerful.

In parliament, while the usual rhetorical speeches droned on, I sat working on the committee's report. The report needed to be written with clarity, avoid red herrings, and propose solutions. I wrote that the committee's hearings started from the same premise as government in its 2000–2005 plan: that HIV causes AIDS. Our conclusion was that South Africa needed to respond holistically on prevention and treatment. Government's response needed to be informed and driven by people living with Aids and it had to tackle HIV/Aids, poverty, and gender-based violence. The key was addressing gender inequalities evident in economic, political and social disparity.

In parliament the ANC chief whip finally confirmed that our report on HIV/Aids would be dealt with in the ANC's special caucus workshop at the weekend of 10 and 11 November. Beforehand I presented the report to an ANC 'chairs of committees' meeting. Very few chairs attended but at least there was some support for our recommendations to take to the caucus workshop. I also canvassed for support among a few other significant ANC members.

I knew that every member of the caucus needed to see this report, even though the chief whip told me it was only necessary to make three copies, one for the chair of each of the workshop's commissions. On the day, an ANC staff member kindly volunteered

to get to work at 5 am to make copies for everyone. When the workshop began, every single MP received a copy. President Mbeki did not attend. The health minister spoke for a very long time and said nothing we had not heard before. There was very little time left for me to deal with the committee's report.

When Tshabalala-Msimang finally finished, a woman MP moved that 'Since Comrade Manto has already covered the question of HIV/Aids, there is no need to spend any more time having Comrade Pregs do another presentation on HIV/Aids.' Many voices interrupted her, insisting that they wanted to hear, and the chair gave me permission to proceed. I kept focused on the report; there was little time to capture the essence. At the end a spontaneous burst of applause and a tangible sense of relief filled the room. The whip announced that the report would be discussed in the commission on HIV/Aids after lunch. There were many calls of 'Thank you' and 'You said what we have all been thinking', and quiet tears – many had lost close family and friends.

In the caucus commission on HIV/Aids after lunch, the report came under attack. But several MPs had had enough of equivocating. They knew people were dying in their constituencies, villages and families, and they refused to be silenced. Henry Fazzie, Dr Essop Jassat and Barbara Hogan, among others, spoke clearly and forcefully on the issues. This ANC caucus workshop represented a watershed in that, for the first time, ANC MPs debated and discussed a comprehensive alternative, including treatment, to the denial and fear that had characterised discussion since 1999. Many MPs said that there was no turning back on government's need to provide medicine that would treat HIV/Aids. Shortly afterwards, Ruth Bhengu from the ANC became the first MP to disclose in the parliamentary debate that her daughter was HIV-positive.

Leaving from parliament late one night after the caucus workshop, I noticed that a car which had been parked just outside the entrance began driving recklessly behind me. I drove faster

but the driver gave chase, even when I turned into my suburb. Finally safe in my garage, I sat still, my heart thumping. The next morning I told an ANC MP, a whip who also handled security, about the incident. 'Comrade Pregs, some powerful people do not like what you are saying,' he said. 'The next time something like this happens, call me immediately – drive to the police station, not to your home. Please take my cell-phone number down – and call me.' He was kind as he expressed his concern.

That weekend the back wheels of my car, which was parked outside our home, were removed and the car was left on stacked bricks. Our wooden side gate was smashed to bits. Perhaps it was the Cape's southeaster or perhaps we had finally fallen victim to the crime everyone else experiences. But the timing was ominous and suggestive. After that, I looked around more carefully as I left parliament and as I entered my home.

The great problem was that the debate on HIV/Aids was swiftly becoming highly adversarial. This was the very thing we'd been trying to avoid. We wanted everyone to face the facts together and work harmoniously. Shortly after our report was discussed by the ANC caucus workshop, President Mbeki delivered a public lecture in which he smeared those in the ANC who were demanding treatment, as people who believed in and perpetuated racist colonial stereotypes:

> Some who call themselves our leaders join a cacophony of voices that demand that we produce statistics that will show that, indeed, we belong to the most criminal element in our country, [who] demand that, because we are germ carriers and human beings of a lower order that cannot subject its passion to reason, we must perforce adopt strange opinions to save a depraved and diseased people from self-inflicted disease. Convinced that we are but natural-born promiscuous carriers of germs, unique in the world, they proclaim that our

continent is doomed to an inevitable end because of our unconquerable devotion to the sin of lust.

Mbeki's speech raged at, but did not engage with, the substance of what we were demanding in the committee's report. True, there were white people, in South Africa and elsewhere, who still retained such stereotypes, especially about the sexuality of black people. But we could not waste time reacting to their prejudice or allowing it to cloud our vision and focus. Mbeki's speech reinforced the hidden prejudice surrounding sex as he invoked old notions of sex as 'the sin of lust'. The pandemic could have impelled us to think in new ways, of far-reaching solutions, but this would have required a fundamental paradigm shift. In the face of this tragedy, South Africa and its president could have led the world by beginning to transform the old patriarchal mindset binding us to stereotyped roles and relationships which are literally killing women and men. Instead of reinforcing the medieval notion of 'sex as lust', what would have happened if Mbeki had described sex beyond the inequality, the violence, the virgin–whore dichotomies in which we remained trapped?

In the ANC caucus the following week, the president was present. I came under attack, especially from two powerful men. I kept my response brief and to the point. I explained the political process that the committee's ANC study group had followed. The study group had supported the draft report unanimously, yet weeks had passed without any ANC bodies responding to our request for discussion. By default, then, our multi-party committee on women had met and unanimously adopted it.

Afterwards, as I was about to start my car in the parking basement, Jeremy Cronin of the SACP walked up to me. 'I thought you should know', he said, 'that when they were attacking you I

watched the president. I was sitting closely behind him and his face clearly reflected that he did not like his supporters' behaviour.' Blind followers seldom understand the nuances of their leaders' arguments. On the other hand, leaders should discourage such blind loyalty and clarify their positions. President Mbeki didn't do so. All that happened was that at the weekend the caucus meetings made front-page news, one headline reading, 'Mbeki faces revolt from women.' I was not the source of their story, but those exposed in the article as opposing the report believed I was. Their attitude hardened, making positive discussion still more difficult.

I was determined to take the process forward. In January 2002, while some comrades in the ANC continued trying to derail the report, I instructed the committee clerk to follow the normal bureaucratic procedure for tabling reports. Committee reports that are formally adopted by committees have to be tabled by parliament's bureaucrats, who usually don't keep track of what it all means. Our committee had unanimously adopted its report, so of course it had to be tabled. On the morning before the president took the podium to open parliament in February 2002, while some comrades were still arguing the status of the report, the official list landed on all politicians' desks, announcing the formal tabling of our report on HIV/Aids.

Twenty-five

DON'T MENTION
HIV/AIDS

In March 2002 parliament held its customary debate to mark International Women's Day. That year the subject was 'Women's rights as human rights'. The day before, the ANC whip in charge of the debate, Mbulelo Goniwe, summoned me to his office and instructed me not to speak about HIV/Aids. I tried to reason with him: 'But, comrade, how can I speak about women's rights as human rights and be silent about what is killing hundreds of women and girls every day?' He avoided my eyes and looked at the papers in his in-tray. He knew the truth about HIV/Aids. His home was in the Eastern Cape, a province that incorporated apartheid's poorest homelands, the Transkei and Ciskei. HIV/Aids was killing large numbers of people in his province, many of whom must have been friends, family, comrades and constituency members.

'Comrade, we finished our hearings on the impact of HIV/Aids on women and girls in October last year. We requested a debate on our report then and there is still no date scheduled. When is our report going to be debated?'

He looked up from his papers.

'Comrade Pregs, this is *not* the debate for that report.'

'But then, when will we debate it?'

'Listen, we will schedule a separate date for that, OK?' he said emphatically before turning back to his papers, trying to signal the end of the discussion.

I did not take the hint and leave. 'Will that date be soon, Comrade Goniwe?'

'Comrade Pregs, we will have the debate on the report soon. But not in *this* debate.' He shook his head at my persistence.

I reframed what he was saying so as to leave no room for ambiguity. 'So, I must not deal with the HIV/Aids report in detail now because we will debate it soon?'

'Yes,' he replied, looking distinctly ill at ease. 'But the debate tomorrow is not the time for that, OK, Comrade Pregs? You are not to deal with HIV/Aids.'

Our committee's HIV/Aids hearings and report had exposed the connections between gender inequalities, gender-based violence, misogynous beliefs, poverty and HIV/Aids. It questioned the priorities of macroeconomic policy, the arms deal and war. Yet, in debating 'women's rights as human rights', I had been instructed not to address HIV/Aids.

I walked back to my office in disbelief. It was late and everyone seemed to have left their offices. I collected my papers and bag and drove home over De Waal Drive, my car window open to let the fresh air blow through me. The beauty of Cape Town's mountains and ocean in the light of the setting sun slowly filtered out my frustration.

I could not understand why or how we had moved from clarity to such confusion on HIV/Aids in the ANC. When we were fighting apartheid we were absolutely clear that the new state would have to undo the damage apartheid had caused to the health of its citizens. In 1992 I had spoken at a conference on Women and Power where Nkosazana Dlamini-Zuma had graphically illustrated

how dramatically HIV/Aids would increase. Women and girls would bear the burden: 'When they talk of home-care they will be talking about women,' she had said passionately.

Yet in 2002 our government reneged on its earlier commitment. After one ANC caucus we were asked to gather outside the Assembly to listen to Deputy President Jacob Zuma, who headed the National Aids Council and the Moral Regeneration Campaign. Jacob Zuma is a popular speaker, with a reputation for making people feel included; he has what is called the 'common touch'. We were asked to join him in an HIV/Aids candle-lighting ceremony. People passed candles around our large semicircle. The deputy president pointed to two young people on either side of him. 'Look at them,' he announced jovially. 'Don't they look beautiful? He is so handsome he could be Mr Universe, and she could be Miss World. Don't you agree? They are so healthy and they are HIV-positive. But they are not taking any medication – no ARVs. They are looking after themselves naturally. They are government employees who work well and are both productive. I want you to hear them for yourselves.' He turned laughing to the young man. 'Come on, Mr Universe, let these MPs hear you.' The two young people explained that they were HIV-positive and not taking ARV treatment, and yet were very healthy. It was a crude propaganda exercise against ARVs.

'Oh God, this is sick,' Barbara Hogan, who was standing next to me, muttered. The deputy president of our country was parading young people who were government employees before us as proof that you don't need to take ARVs if you have HIV/Aids. He was standing outside the National Assembly, joking about an issue that was claiming an average of 600 people every day (today it claims a daily average of 800 people). MPs lit their candles and sang the national anthem. I felt sick to the stomach as I wondered what the young people at his side would do when they were at an advanced stage of the illness and wanted to change their minds about taking medication.

Meanwhile, in parliament and outside it, MPs and other friends in the ANC quietly told me about their ill daughter, son, sister, wife, themselves. 'I need to speak to you, Comrade Pregs. Please come and see me in my office when you are finished your meeting.' That was when an MP popped her head round the door of my office. In her own office she had affirmations and poems about love amid photos of the children she cared for in addition to her own, the youngest of whom was a child who had been badly abused. 'Pregs, my own daughter is HIV-positive.' Her eyes filled with tears. 'She is such a beautiful, young woman. You know, I am glad we held our hearings. I don't know what to believe. I mean, the president – I really respect him and I love our organisation, but I am so confused about whether she should take these ARVs.'

A provincial ANC leader confided in me about the funeral of his sister who had died of Aids. 'Those young TAC women were my sister's support before she died. Then at her funeral they were singing anti-Mbeki songs. I had to ask them to leave even though I knew what they had done for her. I mean, this is my organisation and he is my president.' He didn't have to describe how painful it was to ask his sister's friends to leave her funeral. The pain was knotted in his fingers and in his eyes that tried to look calm.

In the corridor near parliament's library an old veteran rushed towards me, heavily laden with bags for her trip back home. She was an MP whom I loved and respected. 'Oh, Pregs' – she put her head against my neck and held me tightly – 'I am so glad to see you. I need to speak to you. It is about my son. He has Aids, Pregs. He has gone so thin. I do not know what to do.' She was distraught. This brave woman had faced down soldiers without flinching. Now she was shaking, her eyes drawn from lack of sleep and worry.

'I need to talk to you, Pregs. I am ill.' My friend, whom I had not seen in a while, hugged me warmly. I refused to believe her. 'Don't talk shit, you look as healthy as ever,' I laughed, 'and as beautiful.'

Her brown eyes pierced through me – direct, excruciatingly honest. She wanted to trust me with her secret. Ours was a friendship born in the days of struggle, over our escapades and laughter. We did not see each other regularly. We did not write or phone each other but when we saw each other, our hearts reconnected. We knew little of the details of each other's everyday lives, yet she knew I would not judge her in a time of moral-regeneration crusaders. She talked about her illness and about death. But just then I could not bear to hear what she was telling me. I knew that you did not die from this illness in this day and age. I could not listen to what she was really telling me. I refused to talk about illness and death. 'Listen, we are going to party together until we are 80, OK?'

Today she is dead. I'm a coward. I did not want to hear the truth my friend wanted to share. I did not want those I loved to die.

In March 2002, on the eve of International Women's Day, I prepared myself to speak in the debate on 'Women's rights are human rights'. Early that morning, before the sun rose and my two-year-old woke, I got up, lit a candle, and sat in silence. I needed to feel a sense of calm. I wanted to reach the hearts of my comrades, to touch the love that inspired the courage they had expressed in the struggle against apartheid. I wanted them to remember who we were and why we were in parliament. When I took the podium, I began with my poem 'Fragments'. 'We no longer see our own faces, we no longer hear our own voices ...'

I reminded MPs of how apartheid had institutionalised violence, including misogyny, the hatred of women, and had contributed to widespread poverty and gender inequality. Now, individually and together, we had to ensure that young women were not crushed by poverty, rape and HIV/Aids in a country where a third of young men believed that 'forced sex with someone you know is not sexual violence' and one in four young South Africans believed the lie that 'sex with virgins cures Aids'. Above all, I wanted to ensure that the commitment I had secured from the chief

whip for a debate on our HIV/Aids report would not be left as a discussion between two individuals behind closed doors. Both the leaders of parliament and the ANC caucus had forsaken their duty to support a committee that was implementing parliament's constitutional responsibility on HIV/Aids. Contrary to the chief whip's instruction, I concluded my speech by talking about HIV/Aids and the committee hearings on the horrific impact of HIV/Aids on women and girls. In the public debate I also noted that our request for a debate on the report had finally been agreed to.

Twenty-six

UBUNTU

At the end of 2001 a baby who was given the pseudonym Tshepang was raped in the Northern Cape. A doctor at the hospital provided her with anti-retroviral medicine to prevent her getting infected with HIV. Baby Tshepang's rape echoed across the country and filled our hearts with shame. Tragically, it was not the first or the last rape of a child. The year before, the minister of safety and security reported to parliament that child rape had doubled from the previous year. Instead of focusing all its attention on how to prevent such horror, government's attention was again diverted. The provincial health department put pressure on the hospital, which responded by issuing a circular that doctors were barred by the national department of health's policy from administering ARVs to rape survivors.

In March 2002 parliament appointed a task team on child rape. Several ANC chairs were appointed to it, including me. Its brief was to hold hearings on child rape and make clear recommendations about what could be done. The task team was potentially powerful. Through policy, legislation, budgets and properly implemented

programmes, the government could contribute to decreasing and perhaps even ending child rape. Parliament had power, at the very least, to ensure that children who were raped were not doubly traumatised by HIV/Aids. We could insist that state hospitals provide survivors with the option of ARV medicine.

After the legal, medical and social welfare experts had presented their evidence, we finally heard from the children themselves. A child rights organisation had arranged for two children from each province to testify. They spoke of being raped by fathers, uncles and strangers. During a harrowing testimony from a young girl, an ANC MP interrupted. 'No, this is not what we were supposed to be hearing from these children. They were supposed to present what was happening in provinces, not their individual experience.'

The Democratic Party opposition MP supported him and MPs from other parties joined in, expressing anger with the children's organiser for 'misleading us'. I looked at the child who had been so rudely interrupted, and the children around her. The MP's response was completely disrespectful. This should have been an empowering process for children who had travelled to parliament for the first time. Instead, they looked confused and intimidated. I put up my hand and insisted that this be stopped: 'Point of order, Chair! It is unacceptable that we discuss this here. I move that we immediately adjourn for a caucus of all MPs and sort out our problems there.'

In the caucus I was aware of the pained confusion in the eyes of the ANC MP who had raised the objection. A courageous opponent of apartheid, he seemed unable to comprehend the brutality of those who rape their children. Though I was sympathetic, I felt he had to understand the impact of his intervention on the children. The experiences the children shared were too close to the bone and required clear focus for us to listen properly. Whatever our own experiences and expectations, we had no right to subject the children to our own confusion.

Before returning to the room, we agreed that our team chair would apologise to the children on behalf of us all and ask them to carry on presenting what they had prepared. The children, noticeably subdued, listened to him before continuing hesitantly. The last young boy ended his presentation with a plea to us: 'My child is your child, your child is my child. We believe in *ubuntu*.' I excused myself and left the room. Alone in the cloakroom, I put my face in my hands and wept.

In the ANC caucus at that time, few openly argued for ARV treatment and no one else publicly supported it. In fact there were several, like Peter Mokaba, who openly argued against it. The task team hung back from taking a stand on the question of children and HIV/Aids, and its first draft report made no recommendations on HIV/Aids. Instead of tackling child rape, it seemed stuck in a political quagmire. In the ANC caucus, 'crisis management' of the public uproar around HIV/Aids and child rape seemed to have replaced the problem of child rape itself.

The cabinet was scheduled to meet in May to discuss government's response to HIV/Aids. TAC had successfully used the courts to force government to provide treatment to prevent babies from contracting HIV. Together with Cosatu and other organisations TAC had demonstrated in the streets. Parliament needed to use its particular leverage. I was chairperson of a successful committee that had held hearings and made clear recommendations, which we had taken to workshops in all the provinces. We needed to do all we could to shift the minds of those in cabinet. From the beginning of 2002, I had met with several ANC members to try to influence government, and the forthcoming cabinet meeting was critical. One of Gauteng's most capable ministers, Mary Metcalfe, had provided important support for our report and along with other provincial ministers had backed the premier of Gauteng, Sam Shilowa, who took a public stand in favour of treatment for HIV/Aids. Cabinet would not be able to ignore the premier of South Africa's most powerful province.

Old contacts also proved valuable. Cheryl Carolus, who had been the ANC's deputy secretary-general, still had friends and comrades in high places. I met with her and shared the report's recommendations, and she agreed to speak to cabinet members with whom she had worked in the UDF in the 1980s. I even made contact with the wife of a cabinet minister. She was passionate as she promised to draw up a memo for her husband: 'If he does not stand up in cabinet,' she laughed, 'I will divorce him!'

Together, we must have all made a difference. In the month I resigned from parliament, cabinet committed the government to the committee's key recommendations on treatment; to prevent parent-to-child transmission, for post-exposure prophylaxis after rape, and to pursue affordable medicine for all who needed it. However, between cabinet's statement and its implementation lay a vast swamp of confusion. That confusion can no longer drag government away from a core responsibility to challenge the international trade regime so that it can provide free health care for its poorest citizens, including affordable generic medicine for HIV/Aids.

CONCLUSION

After I handed in my letter of resignation, the ANC issued a statement to say that I had retired from parliament. True, I'd lived a full life, but I was far from retirement age. I had enjoyed my eight years as an ANC MP working to improve the quality of life and status of women. But the arms deal and HIV/Aids were a brick wall. The soul-destroying response to child rape was the final straw.

From 1994 everyone who left our democratic parliament (including those responsible for apartheid's worst violence) was allowed to participate in one or other debate as public farewell and thanks to the National Assembly and to the people of South Africa. I was eventually scheduled to speak in a debate in my final week but was informed the day before that this decision had been changed and it was no longer possible for me to address the Assembly before I left.

Members of the study group of the committee on women planned a farewell, which they wanted to host at the luxurious Mount Nelson Hotel. When I heard, I refused to sanction spending

any committee funds on it. We would hold the function in the old Assembly dining-room, for free. I insisted that I would pay for the catering, which would be tasty but simple. Several members, exasperated by this frugality, were relieved when the committee's secretary, Kim Davids, secured a donation of wine. We were to meet up after the parliamentary debates on the evening of 30 May 2002.

On that last day, the committee's massive report on violence against women was tabled. It was to prove its worth. Later that year after I had spoken at a meeting that was part of the United Nations world summit on social security and development, Cheryl Gillwald, the efficient deputy minister of justice, stood up from the floor. 'In my bag are my two bibles. One of them is the Constitution and the other is Pregs's report on violence against women.' I had edited the report through my pregnancy and after it, with the help of several researchers, especially a dedicated volunteer, Melissa Fourie, and parliamentary researchers Shereen Dawood and Carmine Rustin. It reviewed our work on gender-based violence including our controversial hearings in 1999, and made clear recommendations in each area. I had been determined to get it tabled before I left, to ensure that it contributed to the changes women needed, and was glad to hear that Cheryl was using it.

In my last ANC caucus on 30 May, I was pleasantly surprised at the end when the chair said, almost as an afterthought, 'Comrades, we have about five minutes left so we can allow Comrade Pregs, who is leaving us, to say some few words. Comrade Pregs, you can come up.' Weeks before, I had asked to take leave of my comrades in caucus as well as the National Assembly but had received no response. I had drafted something for that evening's farewell but now I didn't have it with me. Still, I'd been given a welcome invitation. As I walked forward in my grandmother's sari, I breathed deeply, calming myself, preparing to speak. I was aware of those who avoided my eyes, as if I no longer existed. I began

with my favourite saying, 'Tell no lies, claim no easy victories', and thanked the ANC and my comrades as I reiterated my position on HIV/Aids and the arms deal.

As I walked back to my seat, Peter Mokaba, who had argued against anti-retroviral treatment for HIV/Aids, stood up. He reached out to me. 'Keep on telling the truth, Comrade Pregs.' It was the last time I saw Peter alive. He died shortly afterwards, reportedly from Aids.

In the evening the old Assembly dining-room was packed. I was moved to see that almost all of the veteran women MPs were waiting patiently in their seats instead of taking the early bus home. Almost everyone from the committee on women was there, as well as many members of the ANC women's caucus. Lindiwe Sisulu, sharp, compassionate and stylish, stood at the back of the room – the only cabinet minister I spotted.

Paul held our youngest child, Saien, in his arms, as he addressed the crowd with characteristic understatement. He spoke of 'the integrity Pregs lives life with' in one sentence and then shared a poem that he delivered in his dry, slightly droll manner that had everyone in stitches. He claimed that the poem had been written by our two-year-old Saien: 'Eight years in this house seems a long time to me; I spent nine months here and I couldn't wait to be free.'

Frene Ginwala, the Speaker of the National Assembly, began by saying that she had come intending to persuade me not to leave, but she ended by reminding me that the door I left through was a revolving one and I was always welcome back. She added that those present were not those who usually came into parliament's corridors to make deals and rub shoulders with VIPs. 'You know, all the rest of us talk about opening the doors of parliament to the people. Pregs makes it happen.' It touched me deeply that Frene, despite all our differences, had recognised my attempts to contribute to our vision of what our parliament should be.

My daughter Parusha, tall and beautiful, spoke for herself and Yashodan. Her quick wit enchanted the room. She spoke as if she was entertaining us at home and had everyone sitting up at her direct honesty. 'Ma, you know I've always loved you, but it's only recently that I've started to like you.' She had everyone in stitches over my habits that she'd found strange in childhood. My sitting cross-legged in restaurants was one of the worst. And how she'd wished that I would discipline Yashodan and her by giving them a hiding and getting it over with rather than telling them to go and sit quietly. ('Think about how you can play without hurting each other. Come back and tell me when you've decided how to behave differently.') She ended by saying what I had meant to her. 'Tonight everyone has spoken about my mother's contributions to trying to end poverty and to the women of South Africa. I know her as my mother, the person I could rely on to drop everything to be there for me whenever I needed her.'

None of the accolades meant more to me than Parusha's. I had entered parliament while fighting a claim for split custody that had been the most painful challenge of my life. Amid her teasing words at my farewell, which evoked raucous laughter, my daughter's tribute cut through my failures and insecurities, as she gently, playfully touched my heart. When I finally stood up to speak, wearing my grandmother's sari, I felt joyous, free, held by love.

AFTERWORD

After leaving parliament I'd planned to sit, reflect and write. I reflected and I wrote – I wrote and I wrote. And I ran from the pain that the words unfurled. I worked harder than ever in the activism I was used to, around South Africa and internationally.

At an international meeting in Kerala on gender and institutional transformation, I honoured the often devalued and invisible contribution of all women to our world:

> Power and politics have traditionally been the domain of our fathers and grandfathers. I stand here today in my grandmother's sari – a woman who was a midwife and market gardener who was widowed young with four sons and my mother. I decided to wear it to honour her power, and the power of all our grandmothers, mothers and sisters who tried to enter the 'traditional' domains of power outside their homes. Women who had tried to do this while remaining whole and intact – in a world that has very little respect for women, especially poor and working-class women.

I ended by saying:

> I have not left power, nor have I left politics. It is critical
> for each one of us to recognise, to value and to respect our
> own agency, our own power and each other's power; and to
> redefine power: not as the power of fear and hate, but as the
> power of love and courage. Not to be afraid to believe that
> we can silence the patriarch in our own minds and hear
> ourselves think and be.

There was an ovation that I found overwhelming. I went to my
room to be quiet. Silent, I heard the voice of my mother's mother
– the woman who died days before I was born: 'The woman you
honoured today was my sister – she took care of my daughter and
my sons. She was the market gardener and midwife. I was the
one who sat silently peeling vegetables. I am your grandmother.'
I listened and wept. In the country of my grandmother's birth, I
had forgotten to honour the woman who had withdrawn from the
violence of her husband and sister into an internal world from
which she emerged only to try to protect children from being
hit. In the country of my grandmother's birth, I had forgotten to
honour her – I had forgotten to honour myself. My grandmother
had not remained intact, in a world defined so much by the
survival of the fittest. In a world where illnesses associated with
the psyche, like those associated with sex or poverty, are the great
taboos, my memory had denied our connection.

Still spiralling, I travelled from the meeting in Kerala to
the Ford conference on globalisation. It was a long, exhausting
flight from India to San Francisco and I was anxious. Two of
those listed as speakers were Amartya Sen and Joseph Stiglitz,
Nobel Prize winners in economics. I was supposed to describe
the South African experience. I had been working on this for

weeks, reading all the material on the subject that I could lay my hands on, writing and rewriting. In the Ford participants' file was a speech I had presented to the Commission on Globalisation entitled 'Globalisation through women's eyes'. I had written it in December 2001, shortly after writing the committee's report on HIV/Aids. At the last minute I decided that this was the speech I needed to present, and put away my notes on the South African experience.

Despite having made my mind up, I was still anxious. When Gerry Salole, the convener, introduced me as one of the most courageous women he knew, I felt the bottom fall out of my chair. I wanted to be anywhere but on that stage. I wanted to whisper to Gerry that I was not courageous ... that I had felt fear each time I stood up, each time I looked around and there was no one else standing with me – even though I knew that millions who were not in that particular space wanted the same thing that I was standing up for, and that I was duty-bound to use my voice and access. None of that counted in that moment. I wanted to belong, to stop being the outsider. Like everyone else, I too wanted to be loved. I felt afraid.

The walk from my seat to the podium took every ounce of concentration. I drew on my years of meditation, of yogic breathing, to let go of the fear, to calm and focus myself to speak about the women and girls, the working poor, filling the sweatshops of billionaires who stride the globe. There were many who loved what I said, who stopped me afterwards in the lifts and corridors, held me as they said that this was what we needed, this world-view that recognised the power and agency of every single human being.

There was a single dismissive criticism that labelled my words 'surreal'. I came back home, having forgotten all the appreciative comments. Perhaps it was surreal to believe that the lives of the poorest and most powerless could be honoured, recognised and respected in

the world of power. Perhaps it was surreal to try to assert that power could be based on love, not hate, fear or greed. I was exhausted and too ill to remember what was positive. I knew it was time to take care of myself. Reflecting and writing on my own life experience was the hardest thing I had ever done. It peeled back memories, layer upon layer, some too painful to spend time contemplating. Each time, I had to keep relearning the lesson that nothing was too painful not to be sat with, walked with, danced through, looked at and held without fear, suppression or harsh judgement.

The easy verdict about people like me is that we teach best what we most yearn for. Perhaps that is true. I taught others about the power within the self and saw magic happen as people discarded the terrible messages they had internalised about themselves. While I experienced happiness and peace of mind through my meditation and was able to take this into my work and share it with others, I struggled to maintain this power consistently within myself. I was often overcome with self-doubt and insecurity. Perhaps it was true that I was throwing my energy into the world and its pain because I was running from my own. But I knew that the simple equation which reduced the hard work itself to the problem was not correct.

Over the next few years I continued to work, using writing and education. I wrote of what women experienced, as a result of neo-liberal economic policies, HIV/Aids, war, rape, secrecy and silence. Tired of being designated 'ex-MP', I named what I did with an acronym whose implicit insubordination amused me late one full-moon night: Women's LIP (building women's leadership in politics). I helped organisations develop strategies for transformation and conducted education for leaders in parliaments, governments and civil society, linking analysis of concrete issues to an experience of silence in which leaders could hear themselves and those they represented. I interwove analysis and silence with the work of talented musicians and poets, creating spaces to

overcome fear, asserting love and courage as a viable alternative in the world of politics.

But I also continued to engage in direct political activism. Early in 2003, shortly before the United States invaded Iraq, I accepted an invitation to join eleven women from around the world on a solidarity mission to Iraq to listen to the testimonies of women in hospitals, homes and community centres. We listened to Muslims, Christians and atheists, to scientists, artists and factory workers, to feminists, socialists and conservatives, to young and old – who did not always like each other's assertions. There was a rich variety of women, in mini-skirts and burkhas. In Baghdad our team listened to the testimony of a woman whose son had died as a result of leukaemia – sanctions had blocked the supply of essential medicines. Like many conservative Muslim women who take their identity from their eldest son, she wanted to be called 'Um'Allawi', the mother of Ali.

> He was my first child – the first is very much loved. When my son fell ill I sold everything – my house, the furniture – to try to buy drugs for him. It was a slow death, it was the worst. A bullet is merciful – the soldier dies instantly. I fought death for two years. Death would snatch him and I would snatch him back. Death was always at the door, at the bed. I would kick it away through blood transfusions, pills. I did my best to supply haemoglobin and the blood components. But the blockade made it very hard. He was the best student in his class. He was hoping to be a doctor. He would say: 'Mummy, will I get well?' And I would say, 'Yes, yes, you will get well.' He died in 1996 aged 11. What kind of barter was that to take the life, the future of a person? I want to take Bush to court. Who is the lawyer who will defend him against so many thousands of women who suffer because of him? He killed my son.

She cried bitterly as she spoke. 'I don't want your tears,' she said to us. 'Take my voice and spread it in the whole world. I want to hear the echo of what you do.'

◎

In 2004, the 'war against terror' was not over and most governments, including my own, had long since fallen in line with economic trends set by the US government, which increased defence budgets, valuing war and profit over peace and life. There was a frightening increase in religious and economic fundamentalism and violence in Iraq, in the US and across the world. Iraqi women faced violence, from foreign soldiers and, like American women, from men in their own homes and neighbourhoods. President Bush and Prime Minister Blair continued to spin lies about weapons of mass destruction, despite all evidence to the contrary. In South Africa we continued to suffer the confusion around HIV/Aids, the arms deal had begun tearing the ANC apart, and every day new stories of the horrific violence against women and children seeped out of homes and into the media.

I was burnt out from my work. Just before my birthday I decided to take two creative days in solitude, to meditate, reflect and write. It was late in the evening when I finally left Cape Town and my family behind. The next morning I woke early and took a long walk on a beach bathed in an orange-pink sunrise. Back at the holiday apartment, I did an hour's yoga before calling home. Paul answered the phone sleepily and wished me happy birthday, and Saien gave up his Lego, bounded over and merrily chatted until Lego reclaimed him.

I put the phone down and played some Native Canadian music that had been a gift from Marilyn Buffalo, president of the Native Women's Association of Canada, whom I had met in late 1998 when I visited Canada as part of Madiba's delegation. My bag had been lost en route and I had had to buy some clothes. Marilyn

came with me and I laughed as she urged me to get strong boots 'to kick ass with'. By birth, Marilyn was a chief and planned to claim this right – she was sick of the men who sold out the rights of her people. On my birthday I danced naked to Marilyn's music after giving myself an ayurvedic oil massage.

Outside, the world began to stir. People arrived for their morning walk before work; mothers, fathers and minders pushed children in prams; sweating joggers and cyclists went the extra mile. I sat typing till about 11 am, when I found a cool spot, relaxed and let go of everything, conscious only of the feeling that welled up within me, making me smile from some point deep within my womb.

On the drive back home, I sang along to Youssou N'Dour's and Neneh Cherry's *Seven Seconds*: 'When a child is born into this world it has no concept of the tone of skin it's living in.' The songs changed and I felt the beat of Africa, the depths of N'Dour's voice, as I wound along the road between the wild sea and mountain. I'd been driving for some time and still had a way to go.

My old union comrade, Njengabantu Sithole – Nje – floated into my mind, his laugh, his voice, his eyes and his lanky frame. The last time I saw him was on a Friday in 1990 in the union office in Durban before I left for a workshop in the Cape. We laughed about my colourful T-shirt with its optimistic slogan *Hasta Victoria la Sempre*. I returned later that weekend to the news that Nje was dead. Nje, whose spirit had survived – not in the crude sense of survival of the fittest, but with fragility – was dead. Nje, who through all the pain had not emulated his torturers' greed, hate and fear, was dead. While others had used such power against their own, Nje had worked with the power of love and courage, and together we had weaved magic on the factory floor. Yet, at his funeral I had sung, without crying, 'Hamba kahle, Nje, hamba kahle.'

My thoughts returned to the present. I was glad to be driving against the traffic. The sun was beginning to go down as I neared

home. I listened to the drumbeat and the deep voice of Youssou N'Dour and suddenly I began to weep. I howled. I keened. I wailed. I mourned Nje's death, the loss of his life, the spirit that beat in his heart, in the brother I recognised in the long, thin hands that waved at me and in the eyes that laughed so sweetly and gently. In the solitude of my car, I mourned the loss of Nje and wept for the young woman who did not weep at the loss of a beloved comrade, who did not know what to do with any of life's deepest losses. A lifetime ago I had answered, laughing, perhaps with slight bravado, that 'I do yoga; I bend but do not break'. The truth was that I broke, over and over again.

I was close to home when the song on the CD suddenly changed. Could it still be Youssou N'Dour? He was singing the classic tongue-in-cheek Beatles song that I used to sing to Parusha and Yashodan and that I sing now for Saien – 'Ob-la-di, ob-la-da … Life goes oooh on, La la la, life goes on' – by a group who went to India to learn meditation, to find the love, peace and happiness they captured in catchy lyrics. I was still laughing at the brilliance of this Liverpool song in the African voice and beat of Youssou N'Dour when Saien opened the door of our house with Paul and ran beaming towards me, held me tight, and gave me the biggest, best welcome-home kiss … I was alive.

The worst experience had sent me spiralling. Yet it had also deepened the journey within and awakened love from which courage flowed. Memory had surfaced and, beyond it, a glimpse of the truth that none of us are fixed in heroic or despotic moments of history. Life, as it waxes and wanes, always provides opportunities for our humanity to emerge.

As Saien, my blessing, held my hand and walked me back into our home, I felt life flow through me, like the blood through my veins, like the air through my lungs. It danced through me and I knew that one day I would find my voice. One day, I would let it sing the song of a life not eliminated, of a voice not silenced. I

would finish writing this story even if in the writing of it I spiralled wildly. I would one day release it. I would trust myself as I danced on air.

ACKNOWLEDGEMENTS

Thank you to all those who have been a part of my life, whether as friend or opponent. I have learnt from every one of you.

Njengabantu Sithole and Phozo Zondo, for the inspiration of your lives. May your dreams for our country be nurtured by those who have life and power.

All those who still believe in and work hard at materialising those dreams through civil society, governments and parliaments.

Ahmed and Yusuf (I do not use your real names): this book is not the revenge of an insubordinate woman who was not eliminated but the story of a woman's journey to herself, through the politics of our time and country, of which you were a part.

My readers and fact-checkers: I was humbled and honoured that you would all take the time to read and give me your invaluable feedback, especially in the areas in which you are expert: Barbara Hogan, Sipho Mthathi, Ronald Bernickow, Kumi Naidoo, Amina Mama, Zackie Achmat, Pratiba Daya, Jacklyn Cock, Anne-marie Hendriks, Malika Ndlovo, Paul Benjamin, Ronnie, Kamalam, Daya, Pat and Radha Govender, Parusha and Yashodan Naidoo.

Khuthala Duna and Nomalinge Mbekeni, for all your help.

Dadi Janki, for welcoming me into spaces such as the 'Call of the Time Dialogues', despite my criticism.

To local and international organisations who invite me to work with them, despite knowing that these ideas may challenge their existing beliefs and practice.

The Africa Gender Institute (AGI), especially Amina Mama, for translating sisterhood into practical solidarity. Ford Foundation, especially Gerry Salole and Alison Bernstein: the writing grant enabled me to research, reflect and write on 'Spirituality, Sexuality, Politics and Power', laying the foundations for this book

The Ruth First Fellowship, for honouring me as the first recipient of a fellowship in memory of a woman who was renowned as a courageous activist and writer. Writing and speaking on 'Politics as the Power of Love and Courage' helped strengthen the heart of this book.

The Fulbright Global Empowerment of Women Fellowship. During these two years the Center for Women's Global Leadership at Rutgers University hosted me for two months. The fellowship enabled me to work intensively on 'Gender, Governance and Neo-liberal Globalization' with feminists from Asia, Africa, Europe, and South and North America. This book has benefited from that learning.

Anne Schuster, for your magical writing workshops, initially organised through Jane Bennett at the AGI, with Winnie Byanyima. Anne Hope, for alternating between listening to my story and sharing your own. Pete Lewis, my third son (thanks to Parusha), for taking the time to help me think through, develop and clarify how I wanted the book designed.

Jacana Media, especially Bridget Impey, for your gut response to my writing; Russell Martin, the most dedicated publisher and editor; Priscilla Hall, for beginning the editing process with integrity; and Claire Wright, for excellent legal advice.